BTEC BUSINESS

ASSESSMENT GUIDE

Unit 8 RECRUITMENT, SELECTION AND EMPLOYMENT

CAROLE TROTTER

The sample learner answers provided in this assessment guide are intended to give guidance on how a learner might approach generating evidence for each assessment criterion. Answers do not necessarily include all of the evidence required to meet each assessment criterion. Assessor comments intend to highlight how sample answers might be improved to help learners meet the requirements of the grading criterion but are provided as a guide only. Sample answers and assessor guidance have not been verified by Edexcel and any information provided in this guide should not replace your own internal verification process.

Any work submitted as evidence for assessment for this unit must be the learner's own. Submitting as evidence, in whole or in part, any material taken from this guide will be regarded as plagiarism. Hodder Education accepts no responsibility for learners plagiarising work from this guide that does or does not meet the assessment criteria.

The sample assignment briefs are provided as a guide to how you might assess the evidence required for all or part of the internal assessment of this Unit. They have not been verified or endorsed by Edexcel and should be internally verified through your own Lead Internal Verifier as with any other assignment briefs, and/or checked through the BTEC assignment checking service.

Orders: please contact Bookpoint Ltd, 130 Milton Park, Abingdon, Oxon OX14 4SB.
Telephone: (44) 01235 827720. Fax: (44) 01235 400454. Lines are open from 9.00 to 5.00, Monday to Saturday, with a 24-hour message answering service. You can also order through our website www.hoddereducation.co.uk

If you have any comments to make about this, or any of our other titles, please send them to educationenquiries@hodder.co.uk

British Library Cataloguing in Publication Data

A catalogue record for this title is available from the British Library

ISBN: 978 1444 18695 6

This edition published 2013

Impression number 10 9 8 7 6 5 4 3 2 1

Year 2016 2015 2014 2013

Typeset by Integra Software Services Pvt. Ltd., Pondicherry, India.

Printed in Dubai for Hodder Education,
An Hachette UK Company,
338 Euston Road,
London NW1 3BH

Contents

For attention of the learner

You are not allowed to copy any information from this book and use it as your own evidence. That would count as plagiarism, which is taken very seriously and may result in disqualification. If you are in any doubt at all please speak to your teacher.

Introduction

Unit 8, Recruitment, Selection and Employment, is an internally assessed specialist optional unit with three learning aims. It introduces the functional areas of business and the range of different job roles that are available.

To be successful a business will need to recruit and employ people who have the relevant skills and knowledge to help them remain competitive in the market. This unit provides an introduction to the steps involved in implementing an effective recruitment and selection process.

This book includes:

- Guidance on each learning aim – all the topics in the learning aims should be studied, and the book includes useful suggestions for each. Examples are included, but these could be replaced by local examples from your area.
- Evidence generated by a learner for each assessment criterion, with feedback from an assessor. The assessor has highlighted where the evidence is sufficient to satisfy the grading criterion, and provided developmental feedback when additional work is required. This material provides support for assessment.
- Examples of assignment briefs, with clear guidance on the evidence you will need to generate and submit for each grading criterion, and the format in which the evidence should be submitted.

Answers to the knowledge recap questions provided in the learning aim summaries can be found at the back of the guide.

Command words

You will find the following command words in the assessment criteria for each unit. These descriptions may help you to understand what you have to submit for each Pass, Merit and Distinction grading criterion.

Command word	Description
Outline	Write a clear description but not a detailed one.
Explain	Set out in detail the meaning of something, with reasons. More difficult than 'describe' or 'list', so it can help to give an example to show what you mean. Start by introducing the topic then give the 'how' or 'why'.
Compare	Identify the main factors that apply in two or more situations and explain the similarities and differences or advantages and disadvantages.
Assess	Give careful consideration to all the factors or events that apply and identify which are the most important or relevant.
Describe	Give a clear description that includes all the relevant features – think of it as 'painting a picture with words'.
Justify	Give reasons or evidence to support your opinion or view to show how you arrived at these conclusions.

Learning aim A

Know about job roles and functional areas in business

Learning aim A will give you a better understanding of organisational structures, functional areas and the job roles and responsibilities for people who work in business.

Assessment criteria

2A.P1 Explain the purpose of different functional areas in two contrasting businesses.

2A.P2 Describe the responsibilities of two different job roles in two contrasting businesses.

2A.M1 Compare two job roles and responsibilities from different functional areas in two contrasting businesses.

2A.D1 Analyse the impact of organisational structure on job roles and functional areas in a selected business, using appropriate examples.

Topic A.1 Organisational structures and functional areas

All businesses with more than one employee will have an organisational structure which can be drawn as a chart showing who is responsible for which job role. It will show the different layers of management and will identify who an employee is line managed by. For a large business the organisational structure will show the different functional areas and how they are linked.

Organisational structures

Studied ☐

The type of organisational structure will depend on the type and size of the business. The main types of organisational structure are:

- **Hierarchical structure** – resembles a pyramid, with different layers of employees, one above another. The layers represent the different levels of management, with the most senior manager at the top of the structure.
- **Tall structure** – a structure with several layers of management, meaning that each manager will be responsible for fewer employees. The decision-making process may take longer because any problems have to move through the different levels

of management and a plan to introduce change will have to come down through the different levels.

- **Flat structure** – only has a few layers of managers so each manager is responsible for managing more employees. A flat structure could improve communications between senior managers and the workforce and should make the decision-making process quicker.
- **Matrix structure** – a structure in which employees from across the different areas of the business work together. This structure can be introduced for a project or to develop new products. The main advantage is that the employees will have different skills and knowledge but one disadvantage is that they may have two or more line managers.
- **Functional structure** – the business is divided into different functional areas, such as finance or marketing. Employees will have the skills and knowledge to work in the functional area and will have clearly defined career and promotion pathways. There will be clear lines of communication and line management.
- **Divisional structure** – a large business which operates in several locations may choose to use a divisional structure. The division will operate as a separate unit with its own management and will not fully rely on the top management in head office to make all the decisions. Each division will employ a mix of employees with different skills and knowledge. A divisional structure may be expensive to run because each division will need resources and staffing. Some divisions may be working towards their own objectives and not the main objectives of the business.

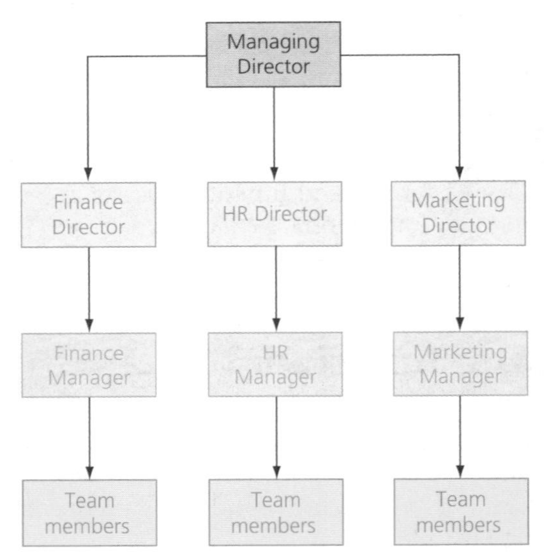

Figure 1.1 An example of a tall business structure

Functional areas

Studied

In a small business there may be two or three employees who are responsible for ordering stock, serving customers, advertising special offers, completing the paper work, finance and stacking the shelves. A large business will have all these activities to do but on a much larger scale and will separate them into different functional areas, with each functional area responsible for one business activity. The main functional areas are:

- **Sales** – responsible for selling products to customers. The sales team should have a good knowledge of the product range and be able to support and advise customers on their intended purchase. They will be responsible for keeping accurate records of sales.
- **Production** – responsible for making good quality products. The team will need to ensure that they have sufficient products produced to meet customer demand, that the raw materials are of good quality and that the finished product satisfies quality checks.
- **Purchasing** – responsible for acquiring all products and resources required by the business and for making sure that the business has good quality products at the best available price. They must ensure there is sufficient stock available to satisfy customer demand.
- **Administration** – provides a wide range of support facilities for the business. They could be responsible for producing documents such as letters, invoices and reports; planning and organising travel and accommodation; planning and organising meetings; welcoming visitors; internal and external mail; storing of manual and electronic files; and managing diary systems.
- **Customer service** – deals with customer questions, queries and complaints. They will also be responsible for providing after-sales support such as exchanging goods which are damaged or faulty.
- **Distribution** – responsible for delivering products in excellent condition to the right location at the right time. A large business, such as Tesco, may use a warehouse to store products and vehicles will be used to take them from the warehouse to the stores. The distribution team will need to plan cost-effective routes and look at ways of making sure that the vehicles, where possible, are not returning to the warehouse empty.
- **Finance** – responsible for accurately recording the money coming into the business from sales or loans and the money going out of the business, such as payment to suppliers, staff wages and utility bills. The finance team will be responsible for chasing customers who are late in paying their bills and for making sure the business pays all their bills on time. They may have the responsibility of producing cash flow forecasts, end-of-year accounts, the profit and loss account and the balance sheet. They also ensure all tax matters are correct.
- **Human resources (HR)** – responsible for the employees. They will advertise job vacancies; keep internal staff aware of promotion opportunities; sit in on the interview process and issue contracts to successful candidates; run induction sessions

for new staff; arrange training and keep records of attendance at training events; record sickness and holiday; and provide guidance and advice to managers and staff on employment issues.

- **ICT** – responsible for keeping the computers and network running efficiently. They will be responsible for installing any new software and hardware such as printers, keeping the system maintained and helping staff with any queries or problems. They are also responsible for maintaining back-up systems and for providing relevant training for staff on new software programmes.
- **Marketing** – need to understand the needs and expectations of customers by reviewing their purchasing habits or by researching what customers want. They will need to design appropriate promotional material to promote new products, including designing posters, brochures or leaflets.
- **Research and development (R&D)** – responsible for developing new products or for improving existing products. The type of development will depend on the sector in which the business operates.

Figure 1.2 Marketing teams think of interesting ways to promote new products to customers

Purposes of functional areas in supporting business aims and objectives

A small business may have fewer independent functional areas, with employees being responsible for two or more areas such as sales and purchasing or finance and administration. The functional areas in a larger business may all work independently but to be successful and run efficiently they will need to coordinate their activities, share information and have clear lines of communication.

Links between functional areas

Some examples of the links between the functional areas include:

- Finance will need to keep up-to-date records on the money spent by the other functional areas. They will need information from sales about what customers have purchased and will need to keep sales informed if customers are not paying their bills regularly. Finance will communicate with HR over wages, overtime payments and bonuses.
- Marketing will need to inform sales about any special promotions or the introduction of new products. Marketing

will need to know from finance the budget available for promotional and advertising activities.

- Purchasing will need to liaise with sales about what customers are buying so that there is sufficient stock available. Purchasing will need to provide production with information on the number of products they require and the timescale.
- Customer service will provide feedback and information (including complaints) from customers to sales, purchasing and production.
- Research and development will discuss with customer service and sales what customer wants and expectations are. They will work with production on producing products that meet customer needs.
- HR will work with all the functional areas to ensure that they have sufficient employees with the right skills and knowledge, advertising and recruiting additional employees when necessary. HR will work with functional areas to discuss and resolve any concerns or complaints raised by employees.
- Sales will provide information to distribution about the delivery of customers' purchases and will need to confirm delivery dates so that customers are kept informed. Distribution will need to provide finance with information on mileage and any other costs incurred.
- ICT will provide support with computer software and hardware for all the functional areas. They will regularly review and maintain the system and software so that all functional areas can do their job efficiently. They may be asked to provide training on new software for employees in a functional area.
- Administration will provide business support for all the other functional areas. This could include arranging travel and accommodation, planning meetings, producing documents, filing or photocopying documents.

Knowledge recap questions

1. State three types of organisational structure.
2. List four functional areas.
3. How does the marketing department in a business work with the R&D and finance departments in the launch of a new product?

Topic A.2 Job roles and responsibilities

To operate efficiently a business needs people who make the important decisions, people to manage the process and others to be operational and provide support.

Directors

Studied

Directors are responsible for making decisions on what the business will do and how it will be achieved. They:

- look after the interests of the shareholders, including providing them with information on how the business is trading and plans for the future
- decide on and establish business aims and goals
- review and evaluate past performances and look at future opportunities for the business
- have knowledge of environmental and economic issues and competitor activity
- identify business strategies, plans and polices and communicate these to senior managers and shareholders.

Senior managers

Studied

Senior managers make sure that business activities are coordinated and effective and that employees, resources and the budget are utilised efficiently. Their job role and responsibilities will include:

- providing employees with leadership and guidance, including dealing effectively with conflict, supporting and problem solving
- making sure that all resources, including employees, are being utilised effectively (this will include monitoring employee workloads)
- producing a business plan and setting SMART (specific, measurable, achievable, realistic and time-related) objectives and achievable targets for all employees in line with the aims of the business
- knowing how to motivate employees and make them feel valued
- taking an active role in recruitment, selection and appointing of new employees
- taking an active role in any grievance issues or the dismissal of employees
- allocating employees with the relevant skills and knowledge to appropriate tasks
- implementing an effective two-way communication channel where employees feel comfortable to put forward ideas and suggestions

- deciding and planning both the short-term and long-term goals for the business. The senior manager will need to decide on the steps needed to achieve the goals and for measuring and reviewing both the processes and outcomes
- continually reviewing and evaluating the activity of the business and when a problem does arise offering support, advice and guidance.

Supervisors or team leaders

Studied

Supervisors or team leaders will be responsible for the day-to-day management of a department or a team of employees. They will take the line manager role for their team and will be responsible for:

- implementing the objectives set by senior management
- planning work schedules and job roles for the employees they are responsible for
- reviewing the progress and quality of work – including checking that the work completed by their team satisfies the business's quality standards
- providing support and guidance on work-related procedures or policies
- coaching the employees in developing their skills and knowledge, including providing opportunity for employees to learn new skills
- listening to any problems and feeding issues back to senior managers
- encouraging and motivating their team.

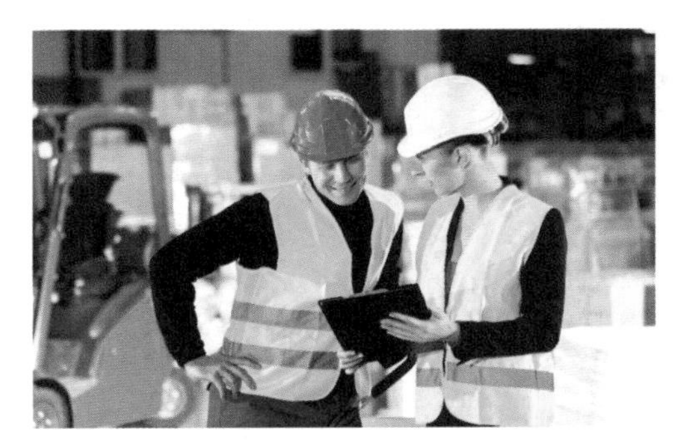

Figure 1.3 Supervisors are responsible for providing support to their team

Operational and support staff

Studied

A business will need to recruit employees with the skills and knowledge to produce the products and sell to customers as well as employees who provide the support activities such as administration. Operational and support staff/assistants will be responsible for the day-to-day work in the business. Depending on the type of organisational structure, they may be working for one manager or several different managers.

Roles in different organisational structures

Studied

The size and structure of an organisation will determine how the business operates and how the tasks and activities will be allocated. In a small business there may be one manager who oversees the day-to-day running of the business and who allocates tasks to employees. The manager will make all the decisions and employees will be responsible for a range of different jobs including customer service, sales, purchasing and administration.

In a tall hierarchical organisational structure there are several layers of management but managers will be responsible for only a small number of employees. There will be clear lines on who is managed by whom and clear progression routes for assistants, team leaders or middle managers. The tall structure may make it possible for an employee to specialise in working and progressing in one functional area, such as finance or marketing.

In a flat hierarchical organisational structure with fewer layers of management managers will be responsible for a wider span of control and more employees. An employee may have more than one line manager because the managers are at the same level and will have responsibility for different functional activities. The fewer layers of management will mean that progression for employees will be limited. In a flat structure employees may be required to work across the functional areas which will make it difficult for an employee to specialise in one functional area.

In a functional organisational structure the employees will be employed to focus on tasks and activities in only one functional area, such as finance or HR. The business will recruit employees with the right skills and knowledge to work in the functional area. The employees will choose to work in an area where they want to specialise.

A business may start as a flat structure but as they become more successful and grow they will employ more employees and introduce more layers of management and eventually will become a tall structure.

Knowledge recap questions

1. What is the difference between the role of the directors and senior managers of a business?
2. What is the difference between the role of senior managers and supervisors?
3. Why is it important for managers at all levels to communicate with staff?

Assessment guidance for learning aim A

2A.P1 Explain the purpose of different functional areas in two contrasting businesses

Learner answer

I am going to use Carphone Warehouse PLC, a large business which sells mobile phones and Elisha's Emporium, a small business which sells soft furnishings.

Assessor report: The command verb for 2A.P1 is **explain**. To achieve this, the learner will need to set out in detail, with reasons the purpose of the different functional areas in their two chosen businesses. More difficult than 'describe' or 'list', it can help to give an example to show what you mean. Start by introducing the topic then give the 'how' or 'why'.

The learner has satisfied the requirements of the grading criterion by selecting two businesses that are contrasting in size, ownership and sub-sector.

Learner answer

Carphone Warehouse is a big business which has a lot of separate functional areas and several layers of managers.

Finance at Carphone Warehouse is responsible for purchasing computer software and stationery for all departments and for replacing things which are worn or broken such as chairs. It is in charge of stock control and keeps records of all the money coming in from customers so they know they have money to pay bills and wages. They prepare accounts for tax and shareholders which show how the business is doing.

Administration at Carphone Warehouse produce letters for other departments. They answer the phone, transfer the call to the right department and log phone calls. They open letters and general emails and then decide who is best to answer them.

They look after the day-to-day problems like arranging for repairs to lighting and are responsible for security.

Human Resources at Carphone Warehouse advertise jobs and arrange the interviews. They are responsible for arranging training and will help sort out any problems with wages or holidays. They make sure that all new employees have an induction and know about health and safety and where they can get help and advice.

Customer Service looks after customers who contact Carphone Warehouse and try to find solutions that suit the business and the customer so everyone is happy. They talk to staff in the marketing department so that they can tell customers about new products or upgrades.

The marketing department at Carphone Warehouse is responsible for updating the website and for designing fliers which are sent out by the adminstration department. They also produce advertisements for newspapers. The marketing department will do market research to find out what customers want and to find out which products they like and why.

The sales department are responsible for selling goods to customer. They have to keep records on what customers have bought and pass this to the finance department so they can set up records for payments.

Carphone Warehouse do not have a research and development department because they mostly sell other people's products. They do have their own network service Talkmobile which came from them doing research in the market.

Assessor report: The learner has explained the purpose of the functional departments at Carphone Warehouse and has on some occasions identified links between the departments. They have not included any information on the sales or marketing departments. To achieve 2A.P1 the learner will need to produce similar evidence for Elisha's Emporium.

Learner answer

In Elisha's Emporium there are not as many functional areas and only a few managers. The managers have responsibilities for more than one function and most employees will work in more than one functional area. The senior manager runs the business and does all the purchasing of stock. The sales advisor provides information for customers and is also responsible for marketing. The sales staff are responsible for dealing with customer problems and complaints.

Both Carphone Warehouse and Elisha's Emporium have a range of functional areas but Carphone Warehouse does have more separate functional areas.

Assessor report: The learner has started to outline the job roles of the employees at Elisha's Emporium but needs to develop this and explain the purpose of the different functional areas. The learner has currently made no reference to finance, human resources or administration.

Assessor report – overall

Is the evidence sufficient to satisfy the grading criterion?

The learner has explained some functional areas for Carphone Warehouse and identified some links between the different functional areas. They have not made any reference to the sales or marketing departments. For Elisha's Emporium the learner has only briefly outlined the job role for some employees and will now need to explain the purpose of the different functional areas.

What additional evidence, if any, is required?

To achieve 2A.P1 the learner will need to explain the purpose of the functional areas for Elisha's Emporium.

2A.P2 Describe the responsibilities of two different job roles in two contrasting businesses

Learner answer

For 2A.P2 I am using the sales job role and the role of the HR manager in Carphone Warehouse and Elisha's Emporium. Carphone Warehouse is a PLC so it has individual departments, each responsible for one function. Elisha's Emporium is smaller so some people do jobs in more than one functional area.

Assessor report: The command verb for 2A.P2 is **describe**. To achieve this, the learner will need to give a clear description that includes all the relevant features of the two job roles in the two contrasting businesses – think of it as 'painting a picture with words'. The learner has set the scene by listing the roles and businesses they will describe.

Learner answer

Sales staff at both businesses are responsible for selling products to customers and for making as much profit as possible for their business. The HR managers in both businesses are responsible for making sure they have the right staff in the right jobs and for helping staff with any problems.

There are two main sales staff at Elisha's Emporium while at Carphone Warehouse each branch will have several full-time and part-time staff. At Carphone Warehouse the sales staff sell phones, tablets and accessories to customers who come in through the door **a**. The sales staff at Elisha's Emporium are responsible for providing a personal selling service where they give advice and guidance on soft furnishings. Alongside selling they are also responsible for several other job roles. Sales staff at Elisha's Emporium have to make sure the outlet is always neat and tidy and check there is sufficient stock for the current orders. If and when stock levels are low they must inform the manager. The sales role includes checking that samples for customers are available and up to date. Sales staff are responsible for taking payments, manually recording details of sales on the computer and for making sure that other files are updated. The sales staff will have to be good at numeracy because they will be responsible for working out measurements and checking that customers' figures are accurate. Sales staff are responsible for dealing with customers' queries, problems or complaints and if machinists are not available they may be required to make alternations or repairs to products.

Assessor report: The learner has described the role of sales staff at Elisha's Emporium but has only briefly listed the responsibilities **a** for sales staff at the Carphone Warehouse.

Learner answer

At Elisha's Emporium the HR manager job role is the responsibility of the senior manager. The job role involves identifying when new staff are needed and whether the business can afford to employ someone full-time or if it will be a part-time employee. The job role includes advertising the new job and interviewing people who apply for the job. At Elisha's Emporium the job role for HR manager includes looking at the application forms and deciding on who could do the job and who will fit into the team. The HR manager will make sure that new staff are told about the business, what it does and introduce them to the other staff. The HR manager will make a record of all relevant information on the new employee and keep the record updated. The HR manager will introduce new employees to the supervisor who will provide the training. Any member of staff with a problem about work or their pay will talk about it with the HR manager.

The HR manager at Carphone Warehouse will place job adverts, interview people for jobs and provide the induction and relevant training on the job role.

Assessor report: The learner has given a good description of the responsibilities of the HR manager job role at Elisha's Emporium but has only listed the HR manager responsibilities at the Carphone Warehouse.

Assessor report – overall

Is the evidence sufficient to satisfy the grading criterion?

In the first section the learner has clearly identified the two job roles and the two businesses. The learner has developed this and described the responsibilities of two jobs but only for one business, Elisha's Emporium. For the second business, Carphone Warehouse, the learner has only listed the responsibilities for each job role.

What additional evidence, if any, is required?

To achieve 2A.P2 the learner will need to **describe** the responsibilities of the two jobs roles at Carphone Warehouse.

2A.M1 Compare two job roles and responsibilities from different functional areas in two contrasting businesses

Learner answer

I am going to use the job roles that I described for 2A.P2. Carphone Warehouse is a large business with several lines of managers and is divided into several functional areas. Elisha's Emporium is a smaller business with fewer managers and where employees are responsible for job roles in one or more functional area.

Assessor report: The command verb is **compare**. The learner will need to identify the main factors of the different job roles and responsibilities in two contrasting businesses and explain the similarities and differences between them.

The learner has set the scene by identifying which businesses they will use and has selected to use businesses which operate in different sectors and which have different organisational structures. It is beneficial for the learners to use the same businesses from 2A.P2 and develop the evidence they have produced for this grading criterion.

Learner answer

My table lists the roles and responsibilities for the two jobs.

	Elisha's Emporium	Carphone Warehouse
Sales staff	Sell products to customers and will need excellent product knowledge Take payment for products. Make a record of all sales Deal with any queries or complaints, giving discounts Keep track of stock, inform manager when stock is low Regular review samples of materials so that they are up to date Produce adverts for products Will often share personal experiences and make recommendations for customers Provide support and guidance and accurate information for customers	Sell products to customers and will need good product knowledge. Can refer to catalogues Take payment for products Provide accurate information for customers

HR Manager	Produces job adverts Invites people for interview and does the interviews. Sends letters out to new employees and people who did not get the job Does staff induction Records personal job details and keeps them up to date Talks to staff if there are problems Checks pay for staff is accurate Asks staff to work overtime	Reviews job adverts Invites people for interview and attends some interviews. Sends letters out to new employees and people who did not get the job Does staff induction Organises training and keeps training records up to date Attends grievance meetings Looks at pay scale and checks that information for monthly pay is accurate

Assessor report: The learner has outlined the two job roles and their responsibilities in each business and will now need to develop this to compare the similarities and differences. The learner may find it helpful to contrast the jobs as well – i.e. what is different about each role in each business.

Learner answer

The sales staff in both businesses have to sell products to customers but in Elisha's Emporium the sales staff have to keep manual records of sales and count stock. In Carphone Warehouse the sales staff do not have to count the stock and all sales are just recorded on the till. If a customer has a problem or complaint the sales staff at Elisha's Emporium have to deal with it but at Carphone Warehouse all problems are dealt with by customer service or a branch manager. In both businesses the staff need to have a good knowledge of the products as the customers are relying on them to give them advice and guidance. In Elisha's Emporium customers often expect staff to give them advice from personal experience about furnishings or matching colours. The sales staff at Elisha's Emporium have to do more administration work than sales staff at Carphone Warehouse because they are responsible for producing adverts for the local newspapers. At Carphone Warehouse these jobs will be done by other departments and not the sales staff. Staff at Elisha's Emporium have some scope to make decisions on discounts without checking with a supervisor if it seems appropriate and will close a sale. This is a wider responsibility than sales staff at Carphone Warehouse where all decisions, such as discounts, are made at head office.

Assessor report: The learner has made a good comparison between the sales role at Elisha's Emporium and that at Carphone Warehouse. The criterion requires two job roles to be compared and to achieve 2A.M1 the learner will need to compare the HR manager job role.

Assessor report – overall

Is the evidence sufficient to satisfy the grading criterion?

The table outlines the two job roles and responsibilities and the learner has used this information to compare the sales job role at Elisha's Emporium and Carphone Warehouse. They have not compared the HR manager role in each business.

What additional evidence, if any, is required?

To achieve 2A.M1will need to compare the roles and responsibilities of the HR manager at both businesses.

2A.D1 Analyse the impact of organisational structure on job roles and functional areas in a selected business, using appropriate examples

Learner answer

Elisha's Emporium is a flat structure as there are not many employees and only one senior manager who will make all the decisions. Some people have more than one job role.

Assessor report: The command verb for 2A.D1 is **analyse**. To achieve this, the learner will need to identify organisational structures and say how they affect job roles and functional areas in the selected business.

The learner has identified one business and its structures and has identified how the structure impacts on the division of job roles.

Learner answer

Elisha's Emporium is a small business with very few lines of management so it is a flat structure. A flat structure means lines of communication are shorter and easier and this is true at Elisha's Emporium where the staff can talk to the senior manager without having to go through lots of other managers. If the staff have a problem or want to discuss a customer they can talk to the senior manager who is the owner of the business. If the owner wants to make changes or there are problems she can just call a staff meeting which all the staff will attend. This means that changes can be made quickly without having to wait for the message to come down from senior managers to middle managers to line managers and then staff. When the manager wanted to introduce new styles for curtains and covers she called a meeting to discuss this with the sales staff and they could put forward their ideas and suggestions. This meant that the decision to include new designs could be made quickly and because all staff were at the meeting they knew straight away about the changes. In a tall structure it may take time for all staff to be informed about any changes and for the changes to be made.

Assessor report: The learner has begun to analyse the impact of the organisational structure and has provided an example to support their evidence. The learner will need to continue to analyse how the organisational structure at Elisha's Emporium impacts on job roles and functional areas.

Learner answer

At Elisha's Emporium there is one main manager, the owner of the business and one supervisor who is responsible for training staff and checking that the work is good enough to send to customers. The manager and the supervisor have clear job roles and staff know who to go to with any problems. All other staff are equal and will have more tasks and responsibilities than staff at large businesses where they only have one main job role. The staff at Elisha's Emporium will need a wide range of skills because their job role covers tasks from several different functional areas such as marketing, administration, customer service and finance. The staff will need a good knowledge of soft furnishings and up-to-date styles so they can give advice to customers. The staff may not be experts in some jobs, but are expected to cover for staff who are on holiday or off sick.

The staff at Elisha's Emporium will have more responsibility for making decisions than staff in a big business. They can use their own judgement on when to make changes to designs or products which will meet what the customers want.

The small structure means that everyone knows each other and they can talk through problems so that everyone is happy at work. The structure at Elisha's Emporium means there will not be many opportunities for promotion so staff may work at Elisha's Emporium to get experience and then move to a bigger business where they can move up to senior job roles.

Assessor report: The learner has briefly analysed how the organisational structure impacts on job role and responsibilities but has provided no clear examples to support their analysis.

Assessor report – overall

Is the evidence sufficient to satisfy the grading criterion?

The learner has analysed how the organisational structure impacts on decision making and provided an appropriate example. The learner has briefly analysed how the structure impacts on job roles but has not yet given sufficient appropriate examples to show they understand the impact fully. The learner could provide examples of how the tasks completed by the staff cover more than one functional area.

What additional evidence, if any, is required?

To achieve 2A.D1 the learner will need to add more examples of how the type of organisational structure at Elisha's Emporium has impacted on job roles and responsibilities.

Learning aim B

Produce documentation for specific job roles

Learning aim B provides an introduction to the recruitment process and explains the role of the job description and person specification.

Assessment criteria

2B.P3 Produce an appropriate and detailed job description and person specification for a specific job.

2B.P4 Produce a curriculum vitae, letter of application and completed application form to apply for a suitable job role.

2B.M2 Produce an appropriate and detailed job description and person specification for a specific job, justifying why the documents will encourage effective recruitment.

2B.M3 Justify how current knowledge and skills meet those required in a given person specification and job description.

2B.D2 Analyse gaps in knowledge and skills that might require further training or development to match the requirements of a given person specification and job description.

Topic B.1 Recruitment

Vacancies

Studied

All businesses need employees with the right skills and knowledge to run smoothly and efficiently. A new business will need to recruit employees but when the business is up and running they may also need to repeat the recruitment process because:

- employees have left because they have found a new position, are retiring or have ill health
- growth in the business's activities means more employees are needed
- the business decides to diversify and needs staff with different skills and knowledge
- employees have gone on long-term sick leave, maternity or paternity leave and temporary replacements are needed.

The recruitment process is costly and time-consuming so if there is a high turnover in staff it is important to investigate why employees are unhappy and leaving.

Ways of recruiting staff

Studied

There are several different ways a business can recruit staff:

- **Job centres** – all the information about job vacancies can be sent to the local job centre. Jobcentre Plus will also provide support in wording job adverts and implementing an effective recruitment process.
- **Employment consultants** – will interview and check the references of any potential employee before passing their information on to the business.
- **Recruitment agencies** – some focus only on specific roles or jobs in a particular location. They will send the business information on any ideal candidates for their vacancies.
- **Internal recruitment** – a business can review their current workforce to see if there is an employee who is ready for promotion or enthusiastic about taking on more responsibilities or a new job role.
- **Advertising** – in a local or national newspaper; on local radio; in a relevant trade journal; in a shop window; or on an in-store advertising board.
- **Word of mouth** – vacancies can be highlighted during network or external meetings.
- **Internet job site** – there are many online job sites for advertising vacancies; some focus exclusively on specialist skills or jobs in a specific sector.

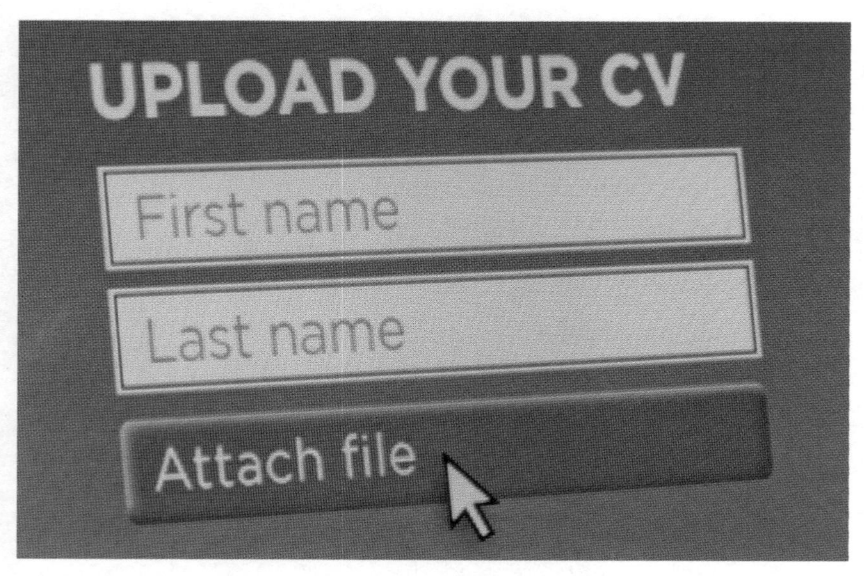

Figure 2.1 There are many ways a business can recruit staff, including using a specialist job site

Types of recruitment

Studied

A business can choose to recruit from within the business or look externally for new employees.

Internal – internal recruitment takes place from within the business. This could involve offering promotion to an existing employee or providing the opportunity for an existing employee to move to a new job role or to work in a different department.

Advantages of internal recruitment	Disadvantages of internal recruitment
Can improve the motivation of employees because they are being recognised for their work	Prevents a business from introducing new experience
Encourages employees to be loyal and stay within the business	A business may not have employees will the relevant skills or knowledge for the new position
Saves both money and time	Internal employees who have been interviewed for the vacancy may be demotivated if an external candidate is appointed
Employees will already be familiar with business policies and procedures	

External – a business may not have employees with the right skills or knowledge to fill their job vacancies and will need to look outside of the business to recruit new employees. Recruiting from outside the business will be more expensive and time consuming but may be necessary if a business does not have employees with the right skills or knowledge to fill their vacancies.

Advantages of external recruitment	Disadvantages of external recruitment
Provides the opportunity for the business to review how it operates and may see the introduction of more cost-effective methods or processes	New employees will require training on business policies and procedures
An external candidate may be more qualified or experienced	Can be time consuming and expensive
	New employees may have set views, ideas and methods from previous employment which may lead to conflict and disruption in the workplace

Cost and legal considerations of recruitment

Studied

Recruitment is costly and time-consuming. If the business appoints a candidate who is not the right person for the job role they will have to repeat the recruitment process. This is not only time-consuming and costly but may cause disruption in the workplace and loss of production. The recruitment process will include:

- producing the job specification and job description
- advertising the vacancy – internally and externally
- reviewing CVs, letters and job applications from potential candidates
- short listing to decide which are the most appropriate candidates
- inviting the candidates for interview and sending letters to candidates who were not successful
- coordinating and conducting the interview and selection process
- appointing a new employee and sending out letters to candidates who were not successful
- inducting and training new employee

A business also needs to consider the legal requirements when advertising and appointing new employees. A business must implement a recruitment and selection process which is fair and not discriminatory. It is unlawful for a business to discriminate on gender, marital status, nationality, ethnic origins, disability, religion or age in the recruitment and selection process.

The legal requirements for employers concerning recruitment are outlined in The Equality Act, which became law in October 2010. Under this Act the wording of the job vacancy must not be discriminatory or state an age limit or gender (there may be times when it is acceptable to identify the gender, such as working with women who have been abused, or age, for example a driving instructor, by law, must be over 21 years of age). The advertised pay rate must not be below the minimum legal requirement. The Equality Act also states that a business cannot ask anyone about health or disability before they offer a candidate a job. Once a job offer is made questions about health and disability are acceptable so that the business can provide the relevant support.

Knowledge recap questions

1. State three reasons why a job vacancy arises.
2. What are the benefits for a business to recruit externally?
3. What legal considerations does a business need to be aware of when designing a job advert?

Topic B.2 Developing a job description and person specification

It is essential for the efficiency of the business that the right candidate is recruited for the vacant job role. To do this a business will need to produce an accurate job description which outlines the job role and a person specification which correctly highlights the skills and qualities needed for the vacant job role.

A business can use different methods to gather information to build and produce the job description and person specification for a job vacancy:

- The documents could be written by a member of staff who is employed in the department such as a line manager or the head of department. They will write the job description based on what the job entails and the skills and qualities required for doing the job.
- The current job holder may be asked to write the job description and person specification before they leave the post. They may provide a more realistic view of the job role and the tasks they have completed. Discussing the job role with the current holder and the line manager will help agree the responsibilities for the vacant position.
- The current job holder could be asked, during an exit interview, by a manager or HR to outline what is involved in their job role and what skills and qualities will be required by the new employee appointed to the job role.

Whoever produces the job description and person specification, it is important that the information is current and accurate.

All job roles change, therefore job descriptions and person specifications should not only be written to recruit new staff but should also be regularly reviewed and updated to ensure that they provide an accurate account of the job roles of current employees.

Knowledge recap questions

1. If a vacancy arises for extra staff, why is it better to ask a current job holder to design a job description for that job rather than a director of the business?
2. What is the difference between a person's skills and their qualities?

Topic B.3 Contents of a job description

A job description should outline the key duties and responsibilities for the post. It will help the employer identify a candidate who will be appropriate for the post and will help candidates decide if they have the relevant skills.

The job description should include:

- **Job title**
- **Start date**
- **Information on type of contract** – full-time permanent; full-time fixed term; part-time; temporary; cover for maternity, paternity or sick leave; secondment
- **Who the employee will be accountable to** – the line manager
- **Duties and responsibilities** – the main tasks and activities for the job role
- **Where the job is located or based** – this could highlight the name of a branch or the department
- **Terms of employment** – working hours, pay scale, holidays, promotion opportunities and training.

Topic B.4 Contents of a person specification

The person specification describes the person needed to do the job. It provides details on the level of knowledge, skills and experience that the person appointed will require and will form the foundation on how a business will select the candidate most suitable to fill a vacant job role. It should identify the accurate requirements which should not be excessive as this may discriminate against potential candidates.

The person specification should include:

- **Attainments** – the level of qualifications, membership of professional bodies
- **Competency profiles** – the candidate's ability and capability when completing a task, for example demonstrating good verbal communication skills, working well as part of a team, their ability to use logical and creative thinking to solve problems and make decisions
- **Special aptitudes or skills** – for example: numeracy, problem solving, managing budgets, HGV licence, competent at using computer software

- **Essential and desirable attributes** – for example, it may be essential that the candidate has previous relevant experience in a similar job role but only desirable that a candidate speaks German or French
- **Disposition** – personality or character such as leadership qualities, team worker, good communicator
- **Circumstances** which relate to the vacant position, such as working in different locations, willing to undertake ongoing professional development.

Topic B.5 Applying for jobs

When a candidate applies for a job it is important that their application catches the attention of the employer and most importantly persuades the employer that they are the best person for the job. Information must stand out to a potential employer and make them want to read it and invite the candidate for interview.

Requirements

Studied

When applying for a job a candidate may be required to produce:

- **Application form** – this should explain what information is required and how it should be presented. Electronically generated forms look more professional than handwritten forms but it is essential to check that spelling and grammar errors are highlighted. All sections of the form must be completed. All application forms will include a section where the candidate needs to describe their skills and experience or explain what they can bring to the job role. The candidate will need to provide an informative explanation which includes detailed examples on what they have done or what they will do. The candidate should keep a copy of the completed application form which they can review before interview.
- **Curriculum vitae (CV)** – a CV is a list of the candidate's achievements including education, qualifications, work experience and skills. There are different acceptable formats for a CV but the minimum information should include the candidate's name, contact details, profile, education and qualifications, work experience and skills. The candidate should focus on including information that is relevant to the job they are applying for and try to restrict this to two pages.

- **Letter of application** – this is the opportunity for the candidate to demonstrate how their experience, skills, attributes and personality match those required for the job vacancy. It should highlight in short, concise statements why they will be an asset to the business.
- Other documents requested may be copies of qualification certificates, Criminal Records Bureau check (CRB) (for jobs involving children or vulnerable people this is a legal requirement), driving licence or passport.
- The candidate may be required to sit pre-application tests such as online psychometric tests, a physical fitness test, sight test or health checks which are relevant to the job.

Next steps

Studied

Once the candidate has submitted the necessary documents they will have to wait until the business decides whether they have been successful and reached the next step in the recruitment and selection process. The next steps will include:

- **Shortlisting** – this will involve reading application forms, CVs or letters of application and deciding on which candidates to invite for interview. The employer will also look at the essential and desirable attributes in the person specification and decide which candidates have the necessary attributes for the role.
- **Invitation to interview** – once the employer has decided on which candidates to invite for interview, invitations to the interviews should be despatched. Most invitations are sent by letter, which provides information on the interview process and what the candidates are required to bring with them. Traditionally the interview will be face to face but some initial interviews are conducted over the telephone. If the telephone interview is successful the candidate will be invited to a face-to-face interview. Candidates are likely to be interviewed by more than one member of staff and asked questions which assess their suitability for the new job role. In most structured interview procedures all candidates are asked the same set of questions. Candidates will get the opportunity

Figure 2.2 Employees will look at the job application forms before shortlisting candidates to ask the panel questions about the business and the work procedures. This will allow them to decide if they want to work for the business.

- A business could choose to use an **assessment process**, as well as or instead of an interview, to identify the right candidate for the job. The assessment process could be a test, a relevant case study or a presentation. Candidates are often asked to present a slideshow presentation which focuses on one or two aspects of the job role. The candidates should be informed about the type of assessment process in the letter inviting them to interview.
- A business could use **skills-based assessment** by way of a practical task if that is appropriate to the job. An example would be for a motor mechanic.
- **Feedback** – if the candidate is unsuccessful they can request feedback from the employer on why they were not appointed. The request for feedback will be beneficial for any future job applications.
- The successful candidate will be offered the job and issued with a contract of employment.

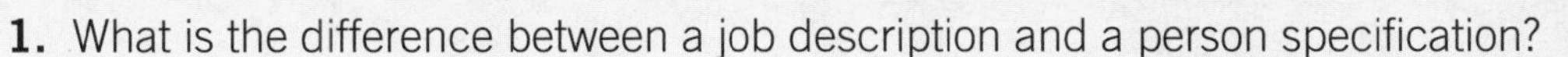

Knowledge recap questions

1. What is the difference between a job description and a person specification?
2. Why would an employer put a start date and contract basis on a job description?
3. Why would an employer want specific qualifications recorded on the person specification?
4. What is the difference between essential and desirable attributes?
5. What is a CV?
6. Why would an employer ask for people to apply via an application form rather than via a letter and CV?
7. What would be the benefits of asking for a handwritten letter of application and a CV?
8. Why do businesses such as the Fire Service carry out pre-application fitness tests?

Assessment guidance for learning aim B

2B.P3 Produce an appropriate and detailed job description and person specification for a specific job

Learner answer

I have decided to use a Customer Service Assistant job role for 2B.P3 because this is what I am interested in doing. I will need to produce a job description for the Customer Service Assistant and then the person specification.

Assessor report: The command verb for 2B.P3 is **produce**. To achieve 2B.P3 the learner will need to provide a detailed job description and person specification for a specific job. The learner has set the scene by identifying an appropriate job role and by identifying the documents they will need to produce.

Learner answer

This is my job description for a Customer Service Assistant.

Job description	
Job title	Customer Service Assistant
Location	Customer Service Department – TA Walton Department Store
Reports to	Customer Service Support Team Leader
Hours of work	39 hours per week over five days, which includes Saturday and Sunday (worked on a rota)
Pay scale	£6.25 per hour
Job outline	To help resolve customer enquires both face to face and on the telephone in a prompt and professional manner, ensuring high standards of customer service are delivered.

Key responsibilities and duties
1. To answer the telephone in a prompt and polite manner, listening to the customer enquiry, where possible answering the enquiry or arranging for another member of staff to contact the customer.
2. Work on the main customer service support desk greeting customers and listening to customer enquiries. Where possible answering enquiries or arranging for another member of staff to meet with the customer.
3. Completion of the online record for all customer queries. Email document to relevant department.
4. On daily basis update the main spreadsheets with information about customer queries and email to the Customer Service Team Leader before the end of the day.
5. Carry out any other administration duties as requested by Team Leaders or Management.
6. Adhere to all policies, including health and safety.
7. Work as a member of the team.
8. Attend all training and take responsibility for personal development.

Assessor report: The learner has included information on the job title, the location, line management and the main responsibilities but has not included information on the type of contract. People who want to apply for the position will want to know if the job is full or part-time and whether the position is permanent or temporary.

 Learner answer

This is my person specification.

Person Specification – Customer Service Assistant		
Essential	Desirable	Method of Assessment
Good standard of education GCSE grade C or above or equivalent in English and mathematics		Application form/CV Interview
Demonstrate good customer service skills Experience in a customer service role	NVQ Level 2 in Customer Service or Business Administration	Application form/CV Interview
Excellent verbal and written communication skills which include active listening skills		Application form/CV Interview
Friendly, polite and approachable both on the telephone and face to face		Application form /CV Interview

Smart appearance		Interview
Team player		Application form/CV Interview
Administration skills	NVQ Level 2 in Customer Service or Business Administration	Interview Pre-selection test
Willing to attend regular training programmes		Application form/CV Interview
Good organisational and time management skills		Application form/CV Interview
Ability to stay calm and work under pressure		Application form/CV Interview
Ability to deal with customer enquiries in a clear manner		Application form/CV Interview
Previous experience of spreadsheets	IT qualification including spreadsheets	Application form/CV Interview
Emailing – both sending, forwarding and replying		Application form/CV Interview
Producing documents on the computer	IT qualification including word processing	Application form/CV Interview

Assessor report: The learner has included skills, qualifications and experience in the person specification that are relevant for the Customer Service Assistant position.

Assessor report – overall

Is the evidence sufficient to satisfy the grading criterion?

In the first section the learner has clearly identified the job role and the required documents. The job description and person specification are in the correct format but the job description must show the contract details so potential applicants will know whether or not to apply for the position.

What additional evidence, if any, is required?

To achieve 2B.P3 the learner will need to add information about the contract to the job description.

2B.P4 Produce a curriculum vitae, letter of application and completed application form to apply for a suitable job role

Learner answer

I have been given the following job vacancy to apply for and will need to produce a CV, application letter and complete the application form.

CUSTOMER SERVICE ASSISTANT

FOR

Our **new department store** in Russell Town is opening soon. Opportunities are available for enthusiastic individuals to **join the Customer Service Team**.

We are looking to recruit self-motivated team players who can deliver high levels of customer service both on the telephone and in a **customer-facing role**.

Knowledge of computer systems including Word and Excel are essential and the successful applicant will need an organised and logical approach to work.

Closing date for applications:
16 February 2013

The successful applicant will need to be smart in appearance with an **approachable and friendly personality.**

This is a full-time position which includes working weekends. We offer a competitive **salary and benefits package** with the opportunity for ongoing personal development. Full training will be given.

Please forward a letter of application and your CV to the Regional HR Department together with a completed application form to:

Ms Mason
Regional HR Department
TA Walton Department Store
Russell Town, RU56 9TY

We are an equal opportunities employer

Assessor report: The command verb for 2B.P4 is **produce**. To achieve 2B.P4 the learner will need to produce their curriculum vitae, letter of application and a completed job application form.

The learner has included the job vacancy and correctly identified the documents they will need to produce.

 **Learner answer**

I have completed a skills audit to see if my current skills will be appropriate for the job. My teacher has checked that my answers are accurate and that I would be suitable for the Customer Service Assistant position.

Personal skills audit

Score guide

5 = very confident; 4 = quite confident; 3 = confident; 2 = little confidence; 1 = not confident

Name: Millie Sharp			Rank your skill confidence level (1-5)	Which skills do you aim to develop this year?
Communication	Written	Reports	5	
		Policy documents	2	
	Verbal	One to one	5	
		Within a group	3	
		With customers	4	
	Listening	Active listening	4	
	Presentation skills		3	
Numeracy	General numeracy skills		2	Yes
	Collecting and recording data		3	
	Analysis of data		2	
	Presentation of results		2	
IT Skills	Producing documents in Microsoft Word		4	
	Producing documents in Microsoft Excel		4	
	Email		5	
	Use of the internet		5	
Learning to learn	Sourcing material quickly		3	
	Organisation		3	Yes
	Time management		3	Yes
	Working under pressure		3	Yes

	Working to deadlines		3	
	Problem solving		2	Yes
Working with others	As a team player	With peers	5	
		With managers	5	
	Leadership skills		2	Yes
	Motivating others		3	
	Flexible		5	

Assessor report: The learner has used the guidance from the unit specification and produced a skills audit. The skills audit is fully completed and the learner has clearly identified who they have contacted for guidance.

 Learner answer

This is my letter and CV.

20 Crowe Street
Russell Town
RU52 1OO
31 January 2013

Ms Mason
Regional Human Resources
TA Walton Department Store
Russell Town
RU56 9TY

Dear Ms Mason

Re: Customer Service Assistant Vacancy

I wish to apply for the position of Customer Service Assistant which was advertised on the recruitment page of your company website today. Please find enclosed my CV for your consideration as requested.

I am just finishing my course at Russell College and I currently work part-time in a local restaurant where I have gained valuable skills in delivering excellent customer service. I am now looking for a full-time opportunity to progress my career.

I have excellent communication skills, am well organised and have excellent time management skills. My attitude towards work and working hours is flexible and I would happily attend any training which was necessary to carry out the role.

I look forward to hearing from you.

Yours sincerely

Millie Sharp

Enc. CV

CURRICULUM VITAE

Millie Sharp

Personal Information

Address :	20 Crowe Street, Russell Town, RU52 1OO
Date of birth :	21.08.1993

Profile

A friendly, approachable personality with excellent communication skills and who enjoys working in a team

Education

September 2009	Russell College
September 2004–July 2009	Heathcote School

Qualifications

A Level:	
AVCE Double Award Business	BB
AVCE ICT	C
AS English Language	D
GCSE:	
Maths	C
English Language	B
English Literature	B
French	D
Science	C
Geography	A
GNVQ ICT	C

Work Experience

Verity Restaurant May 2010–Present — Waitress

My main duties involved serving customers and keeping the workplace tidy.

Clive Cards May 2009–May 2010 — Sales Assistant

My duties included providing customer service, serving customers on the tills and restocking shelves.

Reference
On request

Figure 2.5

Assessor report: The learner has produced a good letter of application and CV but has not included any contact telephone details. The business will need to send a letter to invite the applicant for interview and may decide that this process will take too long.

 **Learner answer**

This is my completed application form.

EMPLOYMENT APPLICATION FORM To be completed in block capital letters and black ink a		
Position applied for	Customer Service Assistant	
Location	Russell Town	
Please state how you learnt of this vacancy	Website	
Name	Millie Sharp	
Address	20 Crowe Street, Russell Town, RU52 100	
Contact telephone numbers	Mobile:	Landline:
Email address		
Do you hold a current driving licence?	No	
If applicable you should declare below any current driving convictions giving the date, fine and points received.		
Have you any relatives working for the company?	No	
If yes, please state the relative's name and your relationship		

Qualifications
Please provide information relating to your education, qualifications and training.

School/College attended	Dates	Qualifications (Please list subjects and grades)	
Heathcote School	2004–July 2009	GCSE	
		Maths	C
		English Language	B
		English Literature	B
		French	D
		Science	C
		Geography	A
		GNVQ ICT	C
Russell College	2009–present	AVCE Double Award Business	BB
		AVCE ICT	C
		AS English Language	D

Present employment	
Name and address	Verity Restaurant
Your position	Waitress
Date employment commenced	May 2010

Learning aim B: Produce documentation for specific job roles

Reason for leaving	Still employed
Please give a brief outline of your current job role	My main duties involve welcoming customers, taking orders and payments. I am also responsible for keeping the work area tidy.
Notice period	None

Previous employment

Dates (to and from)	Employer's name and address	Job title and description of duties	Reason for leaving
May 2009–May 2010	Clive Cards	Sales assistant – serving customers, taking payments	Wanted more hours

Additional information

Please use this section to describe your skills, abilities and experiences and why you consider yourself suitable for the job role.

I have excellent customer service skills and enjoy working as part of a team. I have excellent communication skills and a very good knowledge of IT programmes including Word and Excel.

Please declare details of any unspent convictions or cautions or details of any criminal proceedings which are undergoing police investigation.

None

Sickness Absence

Please list all sickness absence within the last two years detailing the dates.

None

Do you consider yourself to be disabled? If so, please detail any special arrangements you may require to attend interview.

No

References

Please give the name of two referees who we may contact for a reference once an offer of employment has been made. These should be your present and previous employers. Alternatively, where there is no previous employment you should give the names of professional contacts, for example: teacher, lecturer. You should not give the name of relatives or employees of the Company.

Name and address		Name and address	
Mrs Jills Verity Restaurant Russell Town		Mr Jones Russell College Russell Town	
Position:	Manager	Position:	Lecturer
Telephone number:		Telephone number:	
Email address:		Email address:	

I declare the information supplied on this application is true and accurate. I understand that supplying false and misleading information may result in my application not being considered or, if appointed, may result in my dismissal without notice.

Signed:	M. Sharp	Date:	31st January 2013

Assessor report: The learner has not followed the instructions on the top of the application form which states that the form was to be completed in Block Capital Letters and Black Ink **a**. Not following these instructions could mean that the application form is discarded because the business will assume that the applicant cannot follow instructions. There are several sections of the application form which are not fully completed such as contact telephone details and the postcodes and telephone numbers for the references.

Assessor report – overall

Is the evidence sufficient to satisfy the grading criterion?

The letter and CV are good but the telephone contact details have not been included. The learner has not followed the instructions when completing the application and has not included telephone numbers or postcodes and contact details for the references. The recruitment process is time consuming and costly so a business may not be willing to invite to interview applicants who do not provide all the relevant information.

What additional evidence, if any, is required?

To achieve 2B.P4 the learner will need to add contact telephone details to the CV and letter and complete the application form in the required format. The learner will also need to fully complete the application form including telephone numbers and postcodes.

2B.M2 Produce an appropriate and detailed job description and person specification for a specific job, justifying why the documents will encourage effective recruitment

Learner answer

I am using the job description and person specification for the Customer Service Assistant which I produced for 2B.P3.

The job description gives information about the job title, salary, where the job is and the tasks the person will have to do.

The person specification lists the skills, qualifications and experience that are required for the job. Some skills and qualifications will be essential and the person applying for the job will have to have these. Some skills and qualifications will be desirable and the person applying for the job will not have to have these but could be working towards them or have a little experience.

Assessor report: The command verb for 2B.M2 is **justify**, which requires the learner to give reasons or evidence to support their opinion as to why the documents will encourage effective recruitment and to show how they arrived at these conclusions.

The learner has identified which job description and person specification will be used to provide the evidence for 2B.M2. The learner has briefly explained what should be recorded in the job description and person specification and how it could be used.

Learner answer

My job description includes the full job title and says that the job is for a Customer Service Assistant and it is for TA Walton Department Store. Anyone applying for the job will know that it is for an assistant role and this would be a junior position in the business. The job description states who the line manager is and this will be where the assistant will go for help.

The information on the hours informs people that the job is long hours and that they will have to work on Saturdays and Sundays. This means that people will have to think about planning babysitters before they apply. If people did not know about the long hours including the weekends they would apply and then find out they could not do the hours.

The pay is just above the minimum wage and this may be useful for people who are looking for their first job or someone who wants to move from part-time to full-time work.

My job description identifies what tasks the Customer Service Assistant will have to do and this will help people decide if they would like to do the job.

Assessor report: The learner has justified how some sections of the job description will provide applicants with information which will help them decide if the job is right for them. The job description produced for 2B.P3 does not identify the type of contract and this will be important for someone who wants permanent work and discovers at interview that it is just a temporary position or a few months' contract to cover maternity leave. The learner will need to correct the job description for 2B.P3 and then add a brief section for this criterion justifying why the contract information is important to the recruitment process.

Learner answer

My person specification lists skills and qualifications that are essential and desirable for the Customer Service Assistant job. I have also listed how TA Walton managers will assess the skills. The person specification tells people who want to apply for the job what skills and qualifications they must have and TA Walton will check this by looking at the CV and application form. Anyone who does not show that they have the essential skills will not be given an interview.

My person specification tells people that unless they have GCSE grade C or above for both English and maths they should not apply for the job. The person specification includes all the personal skills that are needed for the job role such as good organisational and time management skills and smart appearance. A smart appearance is down as essential because the person who gets the job will be representing the business and will need to give a good impression. TA Walton will want someone who is organised and who can manage their own time so that tasks are completed on time.

The person specification lists administration skills and maintaining accurate records as essential because the person who gets the job will have to log information from customers. It is important to TA Walton that the information is accurate.

TA Walton will want someone who is willing to attend training sessions so that they can improve their skills and this is why willingness to attend training is essential. The job description lists the IT skills as essential because some of the job tasks are done by computers.

The person specification lists excellent communication skills and active listening because these are essential for anyone working with customers and especially staff who deal with customer queries and complaints.

The skills listed in the person specification can be matched against those on the CV and application forms from people who apply for the job. Anyone who does not show they have the essential skills will not be invited to interview. Anyone who shows that they have the essential skills will be invited for an interview but will then need to show that they are the right person for the job. Matching the skills listed in the person specification to those on the CV and application forms will save TA Walton from interviewing people who do not have the skills to do the job.

Assessor report: The learner has clearly explained the role of the person specification and has justified why the skills identified in the person specification are important for recruiting the right person for the position.

Assessor report – overall

Is the evidence sufficient to satisfy the grading criterion?

The learner has demonstrated a good understanding of the role the job description and person specification will have in the recruitment process. The evidence for 2B.M2 is an extension to the evidence produced for 2B.P3 where the job description is missing information about the type of contract. When the contractual information is added to the job description the learner will be able to comment on why this information is important to applicants.

What additional evidence, if any, is required?

The learner will need to correct the job description for 2B.P3 and then add a brief comment for this grading criterion on how the contract information will help applicants decide if they would apply for the position.

(2B.M3) Justify how current knowledge and skills meet those required in a given person specification and job description

Learner answer

I have applied for the job of Customer Service Assistant at TA Walton and have completed a skills audit which was checked by my teacher.

Assessor report: The command verb for 2B.M3 is **justify**, which requires the learner to give reasons or evidence to support their view as to how current knowledge and skills meet those required in the person specification and job description and explain how they arrived at these conclusions.

The learner has identified the job role they are using for 2B.M3 and has correctly highlighted that their skills audit was checked by their teacher.

Learner answer

The tasks listed on the job description include answering the phone and talking to customers and my skills audit shows that I am very confident in one-to-one discussions, which will be useful for the job role. I will be confident talking to customers face to face and by phone. I am a good listener and this will help with listening to any problems or complaints.

One of the tasks is to email documents and I am very confident in using the internet and emailing. I know how to send, reply and forward emails and I can set up group emails which may be useful. I can use most software packages such as Excel, which will be needed to record the queries from customers. I can set up Excel documents and input data so I will be confident in recording the customer queries. I can use Word to produce reports and letters which could be required but would need help if I had to type policy documents. The role is an assistant so I do not think I would need to produce policy documents but I would be willing to learn.

I like working in a team and I am very confident talking to peers and managers. I like teamwork where you can discuss ideas and in my job at the restaurant we have team meetings to discuss shifts and new menus which I find useful. I am not uncomfortable talking to managers and this could help in getting to know the job.

I do not always want to be an assistant so I am keen to do any training that will help me move to a better job.

Assessor report: The learner has used the tasks from the job description and the skills identified in the skills audit to justify how they meet the requirement of the job role. The learner will now need to do a similar exercise for any additional skills in the person specification.

Learner answer

The person specification says that they are looking for someone who is smart in appearance and I have to dress smartly for my current job role as a waitress. The restaurant is very strict on personal appearance and personal hygiene so I know what is expected.

Some of the IT skills are essential and I am confident in using Word and Excel documents which will be part of the job role. I may just need training on how TA Walton sets up the documents.

I am friendly and approachable which will be important when dealing with customers who may not be happy or who have a problem. In my job as a waitress I sometimes have to deal with customers who cannot make up their minds on what they want or who complain about the choice. I am very good at making suggestions on how to mix dishes for customers who have special diets and I am always polite. I am used to working in a busy restaurant and always deal with the customers first but at times it can be difficult to remain calm so I may need to look at how to improve this.

Although my job at the restaurant is not just a customer service role I have had experience of dealing with customers, helping them make decisions and providing them with help. I know how important it is to make the customer happy so they will come back.

I am a very good team player and will help peers with getting their tasks completed. In group work I always put effort into the tasks and will help people who are struggling with their tasks. In the restaurant we all have our own tables but if someone is very busy I will help with tidying away and serving. I have not had much experience at team leading but because this is an assistant job I do not think I will have to be a team leader but I would like to learn management skills.

Assessor report: The learner has justified, with examples, how their skills meet some of the skills listed on the person specification. The learner has currently made no reference to the qualifications or their organisation or time management skills.

Assessor report – overall

Is the evidence sufficient to satisfy the grading criterion?

The learner has produced some good evidence so far for 2B.M3 and has justified how their skills in the skills audit meet most of the requirements in the job description and the person specification. The learner has currently made no reference to the qualifications or the organisation and time management skills listed in the person specification.

What additional evidence, if any, is required?

The learner will need to add a brief paragraph to justify how their qualifications, organisation and time management skills meet those listed in the person specification.

2B.D2 Analyse gaps in knowledge and skills that might require further training or development to match the requirements of a given person specification and job description

Learner answer

I have applied for the job of Customer Service Assistant at TA Walton and have completed a skills audit which I have matched to the job description and person specification.

Assessor report: The command verb for 2B.D2 is **analyse** and to achieve this, the learner will need to identify any gaps in knowledge and skills and say how they might require further training or development to match the person specification and job description they have used.

The learner has set the scene by identifying the job role and documents they have used to produce the evidence for this grading criterion.

Learner answer

The skills and knowledge required in the job description and person specification are:

- Communicating by telephone and face to face, active listening, problem solving
- Using a telephone system
- Updating records in spreadsheets
- Emailing
- Administration duties which could include producing documents, dealing with telephone calls and visitors, filing and keeping records
- Working in a team
- GCSE grade C or above or equivalent in English and mathematics
- Customer service skills – experience in a customer service role
- Polite and approachable attitude

- Smart appearance
- Good organisation and time management skills
- Ability to stay calm and work under pressure – important when dealing with customers who are not happy or who may be angry
- Ability to deal with customer queries and complaints
- The desirable skills are qualifications in NVQ Customer Service or Business Administration and an IT qualification including word processing and spreadsheets.

I have highlighted in green the skills and knowledge that I am currently confident with and which are at the correct level for the job role. The skills and knowledge which I have highlighted in red are areas which I would benefit from developing.

Assessor report: The learner has made a good start by clearly listing and highlighting where knowledge and skills have been achieved and where the gaps are.

Learner answer

I am very good at communicating with people but in my current role if I have a problem there is always someone available who will help solve it. I need to become more confident in dealing with customers who are not happy and this will come from more experience. If customers are unhappy about products or service I would like to be confident about the types of refunds I am allowed to give so would need training on the TA Walton policy for returns and refunds.

I do know how to use a telephone but do not have any experience of using a telephone system and will need to learn how to forward calls or put calls on hold. I will also need to learn about TA Walton procedure for answering or making calls. All businesses may have different telephone systems and procedures for answering or making calls so I would need to learn this by on-the-job training or maybe work shadowing someone who is doing the job.

I do not have any gaps in skills or knowledge for spreadsheets and emailing so will be confident in these tasks. I may need some training if TA Walton uses software that I have not used before or the spreadsheets use different and unusual formulas.

If the administration role included manual filing I do not have experience but if it just file management on the computer I will be okay. TA Walton may have a set way to manually file documents and this I would need to learn. This may be where the NVQ Administration would provide the knowledge and help me develop skills in manual filing.

In my current job role I do serve customers and, although I have highlighted this in red, I feel that I do have some knowledge of customer service. In my current job I do listen when customers are not happy but will then pass the customer on to the manager. I need to develop skills and knowledge in how to resolve the problems and what I can and cannot do. I do not have any experience of logging customer complaints or resolving problems and this will come from training and experience in the job role. TA Walton will have a set procedure on what should be recorded for the complaint or query and how it should be recorded and I could learn this by doing the job role. The NVQ in Customer Service may help me with learning new skills in dealing with customers who have complaints but I would need on the job training in logging the complaints.

Assessor report: The learner has begun to analyse the gaps in their skills and knowledge and has made relevant suggestions on how these could be developed and improved. Currently the learner has only analysed some of the gaps in their skills and knowledge and to achieve 2B.D2 will need to analyse their customer service skills, time management, organisational skills and skills in remaining calm and working under pressure.

Assessor report – overall

Is the evidence sufficient to satisfy the grading criterion?

The learner has listed the gaps in their skills and knowledge for the Customer Service Assistant job role and has taken some points from the list and objectively analysed the gaps in their skills and knowledge. To achieve 2B.D2 the learner will need to continue the analysis for the remaining skills identified in their list.

What additional evidence, if any, is required?

To achieve 2B.D2 the learner will need to analyse the gaps in their customer service, time management and organisational skills and their skills in remaining calm and working under pressure.

Learning aim C

Demonstrate interview skills and plan career development

Learning aim C provides an opportunity to plan a career and to develop and demonstrate interview skills. The career development plan will help in identifying the steps required to achieve a career goal.

Assessment criteria

2C.P5 Provide appropriate responses to interview questions for a specific job role.

2C.P6 Produce a realistic personal career development plan.

2C.M4 Demonstrate prior research and preparation when providing appropriate responses to interview questions for a specific job role.

2C.M5 Produce a realistic personal career development plan showing independent research and planning.

2C.D3 Evaluate the suitability of a realistic career development plan using interview performance feedback and own reflection.

Topic C.1 Job interviews

Job interviews are a necessary part of the recruitment process and you will need to plan so that you are successful at the interview stage and demonstrate that you are the best person for the job.

Before the interview

Studied ☐

Preparation and research

Before the interview, research the business and the products it sells or the service it provides. Review the business's website or any printed literature on the business and find out about the business's aims and objectives, future plans, customers and competitors. Review the job description and person specification so you understand the job role. Good preparation and research will provide an insight into the business so that during the interview you can demonstrate that you are interested and want the job role.

Preparation of questions

You will not be able to predict all the questions you will be asked during the interview but by researching the business and the job description you should be prepared for some of the questions.

The employer will always ask if you have any questions. This allows you to find out more about the job role and the business. You could ask, for example:

- What are the promotion prospects?
- How many people work in the department?
- Is this a new position?
- Will there be an opportunity for further training?
- When will I hear if I have been successful?

Preparing for the day of the interview

A good first impression is important. You should dress comfortably but appropriately for the interview and the job role you are applying for. Make sure that your outfit, including footwear, is smart, clean and tidy.

Figure 3.1 Dressing appropriately can create a good first impression

Good personal hygiene is essential. If the job role involves dealing with visitors or customers an employer will be concerned that an employee with poor personal hygiene will convey a poor image for the business. Looking clean, smart and smelling nice will create the right image.

Find out about the location and venue for the interview, how you will get there and the time it will take. If you are using public transport research timetables, prices and the location of bus stops or train stations near the venue. If you are driving to the venue plan the route in advance or use a navigation system. Allow sufficient time for any delays or hold-ups and check the road traffic reports well before you leave. Enquire about parking facilities at the venue.

Punctuality is important – make sure that you arrive in plenty of time for the interview. Arriving in good time will allow you time to relax, calm down and take in the surroundings. If there is an unforeseeable problem and you are going to arrive late then phone and politely explain the issue.

Preparing well could make the difference between getting offered the position and being turned down.

Behaviour during the interview

Studied

While preparing for the interview is important, behaviour during the interview is even more so.

- Display confidence and show interest in both the job role and the business. Be enthusiastic but truthful – never make claims that are not true.
- Demonstrate appropriate body language throughout the interview process. Non-verbal communications will tell the panel a lot about you. Maintain good eye contact when both speaking and listening.
- Speak clearly, in a friendly positive tone.
- Listen carefully to each question and ask for clarification if you do not understand.
- Remember to smile.
- Switch off mobile phones or music players and never chew gum.

Figure 3.2 Demonstrating appropriate body language is a key component of a successful interview

Knowledge recap questions

1. Why is it important to prepare properly for an interview?
2. What is appropriate body language in an interview?
3. Give two examples of would be inappropriate non-verbal behaviour in an interview.

Topic C.2 Personal audit

As part of the career process it is important that you know what you can and cannot do, what skills you have and what skills you need to develop to make you more employable. Identifying gaps in your knowledge or skills and doing something about those gaps is important.

What a personal audit may include

Studied

For the personal audit to be worthwhile and meaningful you will need to make an honest assessment of your skills and knowledge. The audit may include an assessment of:

- **Knowledge** – this will come from studying towards qualifications at school or college, training courses, or from work experience or previous employment.

- **Skills** – these can be technical (for example, computer technicians need to be able to install hardware and software), or practical (for example, carpentry, plumbing or cooking). Other skills include communicating both in writing and verbally; numeracy or financial skills; researching or managing people; teaching or training.
- **Interests** – an interest or hobby such as gardening, cooking or decorating could be developed into a career. An individual may be more motivated to study and gain a qualification in a subject that they find interesting and enjoyable.

There are many personal audit tests available online which allow you to review and analyse skills and knowledge already achieved and those which need to be developed.

Figure 3.3 Carpentry is an example of a practical skill

Matching knowledge and skills

Studied

When the personal audit is completed it is time to think about matching knowledge and skills to:

- **Job opportunities** – the job advertisement, job description and person specification will outline the skills and knowledge required for a job vacancy. Review your personal audit against the skills and knowledge requirements identified. This will allow you to identify if you have obtained sufficient skills and knowledge for the current job market, if you need to focus on gaining more relevant qualifications, or look for a lower position in which to gain more experience and knowledge.
- **Career planning** – when matched against more senior positions in the business, a personal audit will help identify where more qualifications and skills need to be developed, allowing you to plan both short-term and long-term career progression. Planning and reviewing the skills required for promotion may make an employee more motivated in taking the steps required to achieve their goal.

Knowledge recap questions

1. What is a personal audit?
2. When would you carry out a personal audit?

Topic C.3 Career development

Having a satisfying and interesting career needs to be planned to ensure career development is in the right direction. The planning stage should be implemented early and will need to focus on what the individual is good at, what they enjoy doing and what interests them. Focusing on interests will help keep an individual motivated. Not planning or setting unrealistic targets could result in failure. The career development plan should provide the answer to three important questions:

- Where am I now?
- Where am I going?
- How am I going to get there?

Information and advice

Studied

There are several different sources which will provide information and advice on careers including:

- **Careers advice services** – the new National Careers Service will provide guidance on a wide range of topics including: choosing and planning a career; how to find an appropriate course; finding and applying for a job; producing a CV and letter of application; completing application forms; preparing for an interview.
- **Advertisements** – some job advertisements only outline the basic information about a job role but others provide detailed information including a description of the job role, tasks and responsibilities; experience, skills and qualifications needed for the job role; pay and hours; location. Advertisements in trade manuals or magazines will provide information on job vacancies and the skills and knowledge required for each position.
- **Word of mouth** – it could be a great advantage to talk to someone who works in the relevant sector or job role. They will have experience of the job role, work conditions and promotion opportunities and will know what qualifications, skills and experience are required.
- **Careers fairs** – provide the opportunity to meet a range of employers from different businesses who have job vacancies. It is often possible to get a list of the businesses which will be represented prior to the event. At the event you can talk to potential employers about specific roles and pick up application forms. Remember to create a good impression because this may be the first step of the selection process.

- **Friends and family** – may work in similar job roles or know someone who can help provide information on the sector, career progression or current vacancies.
- **Teachers** – will provide relevant guidance and advice on careers and progression routes. Teachers may have developed contacts within relevant local organisations who will welcome visits from learners who want to work in the sector. Careers teachers can provide guidance on the level of achievement and entry requirement to progress to higher education and those required to work in job roles.
- **Previous employers** – will be aware of current changes in the sector and may be able to provide links to job opportunities.
- **Network connections** – people at external meetings and training events will be able to provide an insight into working in the sector and may know of possible job opportunities.
- **Internet research** – there is information on the internet for a wide range of careers and job roles. It will also provide information on relevant qualifications and where to study.

Employment and government agencies

Studied

There are numerous employment agencies across the country which will provide information on a wide range of job vacancies. Some focus on job vacancies in one sector or one functional area such as finance, administration, or human resources. The agency's role is to match a candidate's qualifications, skills and interests to the list of job vacancies.

Jobcentre Plus is the employment agency which is funded by the government and whose main role is to help people find employment. They will provide support with searching for jobs, producing CV and letters of application and preparing for interviews.

The Prince's Trust runs several programmes to help young people get into employment. The Prince's Trust will provide support for start-up businesses and the opportunity for young people to access work-related programmes and work experience.

Developing a career plan

Studied

A career plan will help identify the steps required to achieve a desired career. To build a career plan it is important to identify personal skills, knowledge and experience and how these relate to the chosen or desired career or job role. Researching the desired job role and the industry will help identify the required skills, knowledge and experience and when matched against current attainments and achievements will highlight any differences.

When the gaps in skills, knowledge and experience have been identified the next step is how to overcome the barriers to achieving the desired career or job role. This will require setting both short-term and long-term goals. There may be many options available on how to reach and achieve the desired career.

Choosing between an academic or vocational pathway

An academic pathway would involve classroom-taught qualifications which are assessed by externally set tests or coursework or a mix of both. This could involve moving into further and then higher education and studying towards HNC/HND or a degree in a chosen subject area such as finance, business or engineering. Qualifications at college and university can be studied either full-time or part-time. Studying full-time allows you to focus fully on the qualification. Although studying part-time may take a little longer, it does allow you to work alongside studying.

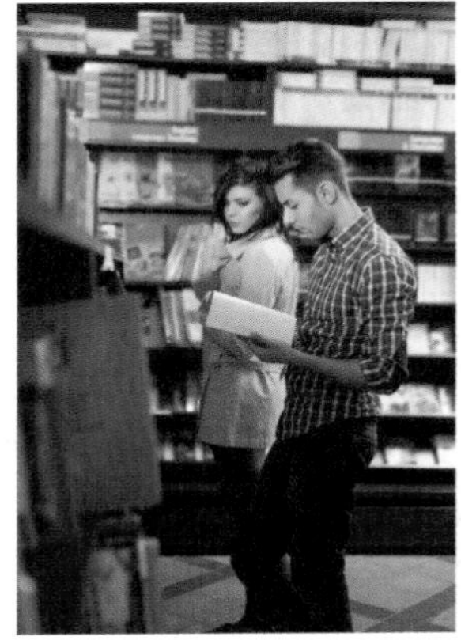

Figure 3.4 Following an academic pathway is one way of achieving your desired career

A vocational pathway will focus on developing skills in one vocational area such as business, childcare or construction. Some qualifications such as NVQs can be achieved in the workplace and are predominantly achieved through on-the-job assessment, although some written work is required.

Apprenticeships allow you to combine an NVQ qualification and a technical certificate. An apprenticeship is a combination of demonstrating skills in the workplace and achieving academic qualifications. The benefit of choosing this route is you receive pay while you learn.

Full-time or part-time employment

Working full time may provide a good income but there will be little time to study towards qualifications or to explore the job market. A full-time position may come with more varied responsibilities and more authority. Working part time means less income but more free time to explore other things. A part-time job role may come with less responsibility, which may be a disadvantage when being considered for promotion. However, a part-time position will provide the opportunity to study towards more qualifications, which could be used to gain more experience of the job role before moving to a more permanent full-time position.

Training needs, development plans and personal targets

The career plan will need to clearly identify:

- **Training needs** – these could be gaps in skills or knowledge which need to be achieved for the desired career or job role. Realistic target dates for when they should be achieved should be set.

- **Development plans** – these should identify the skills and knowledge required and how these can be achieved.
- **Personal targets** – any targets should be SMART (specific, measurable, achievable, realistic and time-related). They should be clear and measurable, identifying what needs to be achieved. The plan should identify targets which are realistic and achievable. Each step in the career plan should be set against a realistic timescale.

Once the career plan has been produced it is important to monitor progress, identify what has been achieved and if necessary revise targets.

Professional and career-specific qualifications

A wide range of professional and career-specific qualifications are available to study at college and university and by distance learning with the Open University. Professional qualifications can be studied either full or part time alongside a job. Some businesses may help with the costs of the course if it is beneficial to the job role and the business.

Examples of professional or career-specific qualifications include:

- **Accountants** – Association of Chartered Accountants or Chartered Institute of Management Accountants
- **Human Resources** – Chartered Institute of Personnel and Development
- **Teaching** – Postgraduate Certificate in Education or Professional Graduate Diploma in Education in Scotland
- **Food hygiene** – Institute of Food Science & Technology

A business may look to employ people who have gained these qualifications.

Knowledge recap questions

1. List four sources of information when looking for advice about a new job role or career.
2. Why should you have a career plan?

Assessment guidance for learning aim C

2C.P5 Provide appropriate responses to interview questions for a suitable job role

Learner answer

I have got an interview for the Customer Service Assistant job at TA Walton and I have prepared by looking at the job description and person specification.
The evidence for 2C.P5 will be an observation statement prepared by my teacher.

Assessor report: The command verb for 2C.P5 is **provide** and to achieve this the learner will need to give appropriate responses to interview questions for a suitable job role.

The learner has identified the job role they will be interviewed for and that the evidence for this criterion will be an observation by the teacher. The learner has identified how they prepared for the interview.

Learner answer

This is the observation statement for my interview.

Learner name	Millie Sharp
Assessor name	Jack Thomas
Qualification	Edexcel BTEC Level 2 First Award in Business
Unit	Unit 8: Recruitment, Selection and Employment
Description of activity and grading criterion	
2C.P5 Provide appropriate responses to interview questions for a suitable job role Millie was interviewed for a Customer Service Assistant position at TA Walton Department Store.	

What the learner did	
The interview questions focused on three main scenarios: What support would you provide for a customer who wants to open an account; how would you support a customer who is unhappy about the service; and what support would you provide for a customer who wanted information on products in the electrical department. Millie was asked to explain step by step how she would deal with each customer. Millie was also asked about creating a good image for the store and the skills she would need for the job role.	
How the learner met the requirements of the grading criterion	
When asked about creating a good image, Millie said she would look smart and her hair would be neat and tidy. Millie said she would smile, be polite and welcome the customer and listen to what they said without interrupting. Millie could identify several relevant skills and said the skills she would need were: excellent communication skills including active listening; good IT skills for updating records; be well organised and always on time; polite and friendly; flexible. When dealing with customers who were not happy or a customer who wanted advice Millie said she'd smile and greet the customers and then ask about the problem. Millie said she would keep good eye contact with the customer and make a note of the problem in the complaint log book. Millie said that for the customer who wanted information on electrical goods she would ask someone to come down from the department to talk to the customer. Millie said she would talk to the customer until the sales assistant arrived and then introduce them. For the customer who was complaining Millie said she would listen, apologise, record the information and if she could not resolve the problem ask for a manager to meet with the customer. For the customer who wanted to open an account Millie said she would provide them with the form and provide any help in completing it. Millie would tell the customer the next step and take the completed form to pass on to accounts. Millie said she would thank the customer and ask if they would like any more information. Millie was nervous but gave clear replies to all questions. Millie did demonstrate knowledge of the Customer Service Assistant job role.	
Learner signature: Millie Sharp	Date: 20\02\2013
Assessor signature: Jack Thomas	Date: 20\02\2013

Assessor report: The observation statement identifies how the learner responded to the interview questions. The observation document provides sufficient evidence for 2C.P5 but could have been supported by annotated photographs or video evidence.

Assessor report – overall

Is the evidence sufficient to satisfy the grading criterion?

The learner has provided appropriate responses to the interview questions for the Customer Service Assistant position.

What additional evidence, if any, is required?

The observation document provides sufficient evidence for the learner to be awarded 2C.P5.

2C.P6 Produce a realistic personal career development plan

 Learner answer

I am currently employed in customer service but would like a career in human resources and my goal is to be employed by a large business as a Human Resource Manager.

I have listed my current job role, skills and qualifications.

Current job role: Customer Service Assistant

Current skills: Excellent communication skills; excellent IT skills including Word, Excel, database, email; good research skills

Current qualifications:

A Level: AVCE Double Award Business (BB); AVCE ICT (C); AS English Language (D)

GCSE: Maths (C); English Language (B); English Literature (B); French (D); Science (C); Geography (A); GNVQ ICT (C)

Working towards NVQ Level 2 Customer Service at my local college.

Assessor report: The command verb for 2C.P6 is **produce** and to achieve this, the learner will need to create a realistic personal career development plan.

The learner has identified the starting point in their career development plan by listing their current job, skills and qualifications. The learner will now need to produce a development plan which identifies the steps required in achieving their chosen career in human resource management.

 Learner answer

I will need to get a qualification in NVQ Level 3 in Customer Service which is for people in supervisor or team leading roles. I can study for the NVQ at most local colleges and training centres including Learn Direct, AH Training, BCOT and the cost of the course changes from centre to centre.

The Human Resource Manager job vacancies ask for people who have experience in the job role and an understanding of employment law so I will need a degree in Human Resource Management or Business for my move into human resource management. Most universities offer full-time courses in Human Resource Management but I found some who offer a part-time course. I looked at universities using the What Uni website and found the following part-time courses:

- Human Resource Management and Employment Law BA (Hons) in London area with entry requirements of 240 UCAS points and 4–6 years part-time
- Business Management and Human Resource Management BA (Hons) with entry requirements of 200–40 UCAS points and 5–8 years part-time.
- Human Resource Management BA (Hons) with entry requirements of 280 UCAS points and 4–6 years part-time.

Assessor report: The learner has demonstrated some research into job vacancies and qualifications and will now need to develop their career development plan. The learner should be encouraged to fully identify the websites they have used for their research.

Learner answer

My career development plan.

	Activity	Qualifications needed	Skills and knowledge needed	How this could be achieved and support required	Time Scale
Step 1	Working full-time in a customer service role	Currently working towards NVQ Level 2 Customer service	Communication, numeracy and IT skills	Study part time or day release Pass the NVQ course and gain promotion to a Team Leader role Support from management	1 year
Step 2	Promotion to Customer Service Team Leader	NVQ Level 3 Customer Service	Communication, numeracy and IT skills a	Start by standing in for the Team Leader and apply for promotion Achieve NVQ Level 3 – which includes a unit on leading a team	1 year

Step 3	Work full-time as a Customer Service Team Leader - while studying for a degree in human resource management	NVQ Level 3 Customer Service	Communication, numeracy and IT skills	Work full time to improve management skills Enrol on a part-time degree in Human Resource Management and Employment Law BA (Hons) Support from management and colleagues	5-6 years
Step 4	Continue to work but look for jobs in human resource management or the personnel department	Human Resource Management and Employment Law BA (Hons)	Communication, numeracy and IT skills	If possible work shadow Apply for jobs in personnel – but may have to move to a different bigger business or may have to take a non-management job to get experience Attend awards ceremony for degree course	1 year
Step 5	Full-time work in human resource management	Human Resource Management and Employment Law BA (Hons)	Communication, numeracy and IT skills	Apply and get appointed to new job in human resource management	6 months

Assessor report: The learner has produced a career plan which identifies five clear steps to achieving a career in human resource management. The learner has not provided sufficient detail on the skills and knowledge required in each of the steps **a**. The learner should have included skills and knowledge for example in: management skills including recruitment and training; managing and motivating their staff; time management to cope with work and study; knowledge of employment legislation.

Assessor report – overall

Is the evidence sufficient to satisfy the grading criterion?

The learner has demonstrated some research into the job roles and the qualifications but the career plan provides no information on the skills and knowledge required at each stage of the plan.

What additional evidence, if any, is required?

To achieve 2C.P6 the learner will need to add more information on the skills and knowledge required at each stage of their career development plan.

2C.M4 Demonstrate prior research and preparation when providing appropriate responses to interview questions for a specific job role

Learner answer

For my interview I have done research on a customer service role and the TA Walton department store. I have prepared questions which I can ask at interview and I know the time it will take to get to the store for the interview. It will take about 20 minutes to walk to the store so I will need to leave home 30 minutes before my interview so that I arrive with time to spare.

My teacher will also submit an observation statement for 2C.M4.

Assessor report: The command verb for 2C.M4 is **demonstrate**, which is to provide several examples or related evidence which clearly support the fact that the learner has undertaken prior research and preparation for responses to interview questions.

The learner has begun to set the scene by identifying that research was completed on both the job role and the business as well as into the time required to reach the store for the interview.

Learner answer

For my interview I found out some information about the store. TA Walton is a large department store which has been open for more than 40 years. They sell over 20,000 different items including clothes, household items, sweets and furniture. Their aim is to provide customers with quality goods at affordable prices. The staff wear a plain dark blue uniform and they have a rota for weekend work. The store is open seven days a week and opens longer hours on Fridays and for seasonal events such as Christmas.

The job role is for a Customer Service Assistant and from the tasks I know I will have to provide customers with support on the telephone and face to face. I have used the internet to research the questions 'What is a customer service assistant?' and 'What are the responsibilities of a customer service assistant?'

Most websites highlight that customer service should present a good image for the company and that role is important because it helps resolve issues so that customers will come back to the business. I looked at other job vacancies for the same position and the skills listed are similar to those listed in the person specification in 2B.P3.

The questions I could ask at my interview are:

a. What on the job training is provided?
b. Will there be opportunities for promotion?
c. Will I have the opportunity to work towards achieving an NVQ in Customer Service or Business Administration?
d. Will there be opportunities for overtime?

Assessor report: The learner has provided some good evidence of prior research for the job interview but should be encouraged to list the websites used. The learner has produced a relevant set of questions which could be asked during the interview.

 Learner answer

This is the observation statement from my teacher.

Learner name	Millie Sharp
Assessor name	Jack Thomas
Qualification	Edexcel BTEC Level 2 First Award in Business
Unit	Unit 8: Recruitment, Selection and Employment
Description of activity and grading criterion	
2C.M4 Demonstrate prior research and preparation when providing appropriate responses to interview questions for a specific job role Millie was interviewed for a Customer Service Assistant position at TA Walton Department Store.	
What the learner did	
During the interview Millie was required, in response to questions, to demonstrate that she had researched the job role and the business.	

How the learner met the requirements of the grading criterion	
When asked about the business and its objectives Millie confidently replied that the business sold a lot of different products for the home and a range of clothes for men, women and children. Millie said the business liked to be thought of as a company that sold good quality items which people thought were good value. When asked about the tasks involved in the job role Millie explained each task in detail. Millie talked about providing support for customers by telephone and face to face and that information on queries and complaints should be logged and emailed to the correct department and the customer service team leader. Millie was asked about how the job role supported the business and customers. Millie said that if customers were happy they would return to buy more products but if they were unhappy with the service they would not come back and would tell others. Millie continued by saying that she could be the first person a customer spoke to and would have to give a good impression of the business. Millie demonstrated a good knowledge of both the job role and TA Walton. Millie was asked if she had any questions and responded by clearly asking her four questions. A good effort Millie, well done.	
Learner signature: Millie Sharp	Date: 20\02\2013
Assessor signature: Jack Thomas	Date: 20\02\2013

Assessor report: The observation statement demonstrates that Millie had prepared well for the interview questions. The assessment guidance for this grading criterion highlights that the learner should demonstrate person preparation and makes reference to appropriate attire. The learner's written evidence and the observation statement make no reference to dressing appropriately for the interview.

Assessor report – overall

Is the evidence sufficient to satisfy the grading criterion?

The learner has produced evidence of relevant research for the job role and the business but should be encouraged to identify the websites used. The learner has produced an appropriate list of questions and the observation sheet does demonstrate that the learner was well prepared for the interview. The learner should have included a brief paragraph about an appropriate outfit for the interview and this could have been supported by a short statement on the observation statement highlighting that the learner was dressed appropriately for the interview.

What additional evidence, if any, is required?

To achieve 2C.M4 the learner will need to produce a brief paragraph on appropriate attire for an interview and should reference the websites used for researching the job role and the business.

2C.M5 Produce a realistic personal career development plan showing independent research and planning

Learner answer

In 2C.P6 I produced a personal career development plan. I started with my current job role, a Customer Service Assistant, and then looked at the steps I would have to take to become a Human Resource Manager. I would like a career in human resource management because I like working with people and would like a job which helps and supports people in the workplace.

Assessor report: The command verb for 2C.M5 is **produce** and to achieve this, the learner will need to produce a realistic personal career development plan and then show evidence of independent research and planning.

The learner has identified the starting point in their career development plan and their desired career. To achieve 2C.M5 the learner will need to show the research and planning they have used in each step of their career plan.

Learner answer

I looked at whether it would be better to just study the degree course but the NVQ Level 3 in Customer Service is for people who are delivering and managing the service so I thought this would provide me with an introduction to managing people. I looked at the qualification on the Edexcel website, www.edexcel.com, and the NVQ Level 3 in Customer Service includes units such as 'lead a team to improve customer service' and 'organise the delivery of reliable customer service' which would be useful in developing skills in managing people and resources.

I looked at www.myjobsearch.com/careers/human-resources-manager.html to find out about the Human Resource Manager job role. The website listed the responsibilities for a Human Resource Manager and these included recruiting, planning staffing, pay, discipline, providing guidance on employment laws. The skills listed included excellent communication skills, flexible, approachable and compassionate, good leadership and management skills, organisational and time management skills, a good knowledge of employment law, ability to work both independently and as part of a team.

I looked at several websites for Human Resource Manager job vacancies and found that the businesses were asking for experience, CIPD qualifications a and knowledge of employment laws. There are lots of vacancies around the country including:

- HR Manager London – CIPD qualified with two years' experience in an HR role
- HR Manager South East – CIPD qualified with experience in a similar role and fully compliant with the latest HR and employment legislation
- HR Advisor London – achieved the CIPD graduate qualification and have level 2 English and maths qualifications. HR experience is essential.

The websites I used are www.myjobsearch.com/careers/human-resources-manager.html, www.simplyhrjobs.co.uk/hr-manager-jobs and http://hr-jobs.peoplemanagement.co.uk.

Assessor report: The learner has provided evidence of research for the NVQ qualification and identified why it would be beneficial to their career plan. They have also provided evidence of research for jobs in human resource management and listed the qualifications and experience required for each job vacancy.

Learner answer

When looking for a university where I could study I found that there were lots of universities who offered different qualifications in Human Resource Management or Business and Human Resource Management for full-time students but less who offered the opportunity for part-time study. I used the WhatUni.com website to identify universities which delivered qualifications in Human Resource Management. I used this website because it provides students' reviews of the universities. There were 70 full-time Human Resource Management degree courses at different universities around the country.

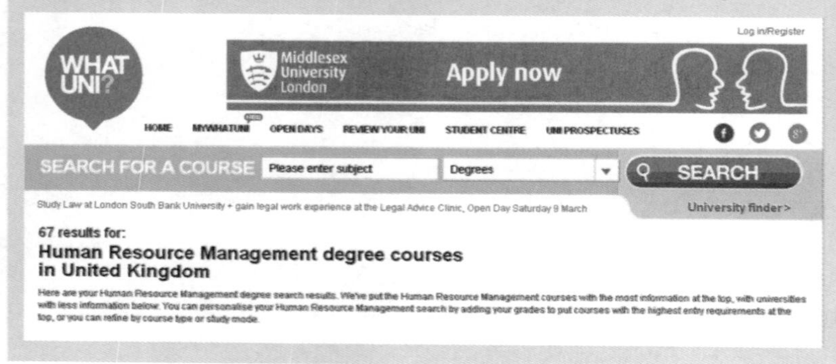

I can only study part-time because I will need to work while I am studying. So I only focused on looking at part-time qualifications. There were 19 results and I looked at the three which were near to where I live and work.

1. Human Resource Management and Employment Law BA (Hons) in London area with entry requirements of 240 UCAS points, 4–6 years part-time
2. Business Management and Human Resource Management BA (Hons) with entry requirements of 200–40 UCAS points, 5–8 years part-time
3. Human Resource Management BA (Hons) with entry requirements of 280 UCAS points and 4–6 years part-time

Some of the job vacancies wanted knowledge of employment law so this is why I decided on the Human Resource Management and Employment Law BA (Hons) in London.

Assessor report: The learner has demonstrated some evidence of research and planning but does not identify if the qualifications they have chosen to study at university will provide the relevant CIPD qualification required by most of the identified job vacancies **a**. The learner will need to check that the qualification they have chosen to study will also qualify for CIPD or insert a more appropriate qualification into the career development plan. The learner should include a screen grab of results for part-time courses on the What Uni website similar to that provided for full-time courses.

Assessor report – overall

Is the evidence sufficient to satisfy the grading criterion?

The learner has produced evidence of their planning and research but most of the job vacancies they have researched make reference to applicants being CIPD qualified and the learner has not identified if this will be awarded as part of the qualification they have chosen to study. The learner will need to check the qualification and if CIPD is included highlight this on the career plan or research for a CIPD qualification.

What additional evidence, if any, is required?

To achieve 2C.M5 the learner will need to check that the qualification they have selected to study will include CIPD or insert a different qualification.

2C.D3 Evaluate the suitability of a realistic career development plan using interview performance feedback and own reflection

Learner answer

In 2C.P6 I used a career development plan to map out the steps I would need to take to become a Human Resource Manager. I want to work with people and help support them at work and that is why I chose this career. I know I am not good with numbers or complicated calculations so I know a career in finance or sales would not work.

Assessor report: The command verb is **evaluate**, for which the learner will need to review the information from their interview performance feedback and own reflection and then bring it together to form a conclusion. The learner should give evidence for each of their views or statements.

The learner has begun to set the scene by identifying why the career path was chosen.

Learner answer

I used the skills audit to identify what skills I had and those I needed to improve. I am confident in communicating to peers, customers and managers but my numeracy skills are weak and I have thought about this when planning my career. I like taking a leadership role but I can be let down by my time management and poor organisation skills. Time management and organisation are the two things I would like to improve and they will be important when I become a manager.

The job of Customer Service Assistant is the first step in my career path and I know that I had to be well prepared and confident during my interview. I thought carefully about what to wear and planned to get to the interview early so I had time to relax. I decided on a black trouser suit with a blue blouse which looked smart. The job is in customer service so TA Walton would want someone who gave the right image for their business and they will decide when I walk in the room if I will be right for the job. I had planned the questions I would ask at the end of the interview and researched both the job role and TA Walton so that I was confident in answering questions on both of these during the interview. I was questioned about customer service scenarios and feel that my responses were clear and correct. The observation statements highlight that I had performed well and this will give me confidence in any future interviews. The planning and preparing for my interview did involve being organised and I felt that I did prove to myself that I can be well organised if something is important.

Assessor report: The learner has evaluated their performance in preparing for and during the interview and now needs to evaluate their career development plan.

Learner answer

My career development plan identifies the steps I would need to take to become a Human Resource Manager. My first job is in customer service and because I had no experience of managing people I decided my next step would have to be in a supervisor or team leader role. This would provide me with experience of recruiting and training staff and in motivating them to do a good job. I would need to be organised and manage my workload because staff would be relying on me to produce work rotas and worksheets for pay, but I know I am responsible and will do this.

I researched the jobs I would like in human resource management and found several around the area where I live. Most of the job vacancies asked for experience and I have highlighted work shadowing in my career development plan. I know I will have to get experience in a human resource department and in my career plan I highlighted that I may need to work in a non-managerial role to do this. My career plan also highlights that I may have to move to a bigger business to get the opportunity to work in human resources and this may be in a non-managerial job at first but with the opportunity of promotion.

There is more choice of universities and qualifications if you study full time but I would not be able to afford to leave work and go to university full time so I only looked at part-time courses. My career development plan highlights working while studying and hopefully this will give the benefit of getting experience in a leadership role while learning about human resource management and employment law. I decided on the Human Resource Management and Employment Law BA (Hons) qualification because lots of the job vacancies asked for knowledge of employment law. The qualification will take about five years part-time and this is a long time to work and study. Very few of the job vacancies asked for a degree so it might be quicker to get into human resource management by studying towards a different qualification. All but one of the job vacancies asked for a CIPD qualification which is built in to some degrees so getting the professional qualification in CIPD may be more relevant than the degree.

Assessor report: The learner has evaluated their career development plan and although the final paragraph does make some suggestion on how the career plan could be improved the learner has not updated or improved their plan. To achieve 2C.D3 the learner will need to research CIPD qualifications and then update the information in their plan.

Assessor report – overall

Is the evidence sufficient to satisfy the grading criterion?

The learner has evaluated their performance in the job interview and the steps they have taken in their career development plan. The assessment guidance requires the learner to update or improve their plan and although the learner has identified the problems with their plan they have not made any adjustments to the plan. The learner will need to research CIPD qualifications and then amend the information in their career development plan and review the timescale identified.

What additional evidence, if any, is required?

To achieve 2C.D3 the learner will need to make the relevant amendments to their career development plan.

Sample assignment brief for learning aim A

PROGRAMME NAME: BTEC Level 2 First Award in Business	
ASSESSOR:	
DATE ISSUED:	SUBMISSION DATE:
INTERIM REVIEW:	

This assignment will assess the following learning aim and grading criteria:

A Know about job roles and functional areas in business

2A.P1 Explain the purpose of different functional areas in two contrasting businesses.

2A.P2 Describe the responsibilities of two different job roles in two contrasting businesses.

2A.M1 Compare two job roles and responsibilities from different functional areas in two contrasting businesses.

2A.D1 Analyse the impact of organisational structure on job roles and functional areas in a selected business, using appropriate examples.

Scenario

Nicola Jordan produces an online Business Education website called 'Princess Publications' where she explains various elements of business terminology. The website is used by students and start-up businesses.

She has asked you to contribute two articles: one article which focuses on the functional areas of business and the second which focuses on job roles and responsibilities.

Task 1

For article one Nicola has asked you to provide evidence on **two contrasting businesses** which are different in size and how they operate. For the articles to be beneficial your choice of businesses are important so please ask if you need support in selecting two appropriate businesses.

Start your article by explaining the term 'functional areas' and then develop this to **explain** the purpose of different functional areas in **two** contrasting businesses.

Task 2

For article two Nicola would like you to focus on job roles and responsibilities and how the structure of the business will impact on these. It would be beneficial to identify **two different job roles** in the businesses you have used for Task 1.

Start your article by identifying the job roles and then **describe** the responsibilities of the two different job roles in the two businesses.

The second part of the article should **compare** the two job roles and responsibilities from the different functional areas in your two businesses.

The final part of the article should **analyse** the impact the organisational structure has on job roles and functional areas in a business. Please remember to **use appropriate examples** to support your evidence.

Sample assignment brief for learning aim B

PROGRAMME NAME: BTEC Level 2 First Award in Business	
ASSESSOR:	
DATE ISSUED:	**SUBMISSION DATE:**
INTERIM REVIEW:	

This assignment will assess the following learning aim and grading criteria:

B Produce documentation for specific job roles

2B.P3 Produce an appropriate and detailed job description and person specification for a specific job.

2B.P4 Produce a curriculum vitae, letter of application and completed application form to apply for a suitable job role.

2B.M2 Produce an appropriate and detailed job description and person specification for a specific job, justifying why the documents will encourage effective recruitment.

2B.M3 Justify how current knowledge and skills meet those required in a given person specification and job description.

2B.D2 Analyse gaps in knowledge and skills that might require further training or development to match the requirements of a given person specification and job description.

Scenario

Your work placement is with the Bolam Recruitment Agency and they have asked you to produce documents for one of their clients. The client, a local college, has a job vacancy for an Administration Assistant and needs a job description and person specification for this post.

Task 1

Produce an appropriate and detailed job description and person specification for the Administration Assistant job.

Once you have produced the detailed job description and person specification for the Administration Assistant job you will need to produce a short report which **justifies** why the documents will encourage effective recruitment.

Task 2

You have decided that you are interested in the job of an Administration Assistant at the local college and would like to apply for the post.

To apply for the post:

1. produce a curriculum vitae
2. create a letter of application
3. complete the application form.

You will need to produce a short report which **justifies** how current knowledge and skills meet those required in a given person specification and job description.

Your report should **analyse** gaps in knowledge and skills that might require further training or development to match the requirements of the person specification and job description.

Sample assignment brief for learning aim C

PROGRAMME NAME: BTEC Level 2 First Award in Business	
ASSESSOR:	
DATE ISSUED:	SUBMISSION DATE:
INTERIM REVIEW:	

This assignment will assess the following learning aim and grading criteria:

C Demonstrate interview skills and plan career development

2C.P5 Provide appropriate responses to interview questions for a specific job role.

2C.P6 Produce a realistic personal career development plan.

2C.M4 Demonstrate prior research and preparation when providing appropriate responses to interview questions for a specific job role.

2C.M5 Produce a realistic personal career development plan showing independent research and planning.

2C.D3 Evaluate the suitability of a realistic career development plan using interview performance feedback and own reflection.

Scenario

Well done, the application documents you produced for the assignment for learning aim B were very good. You have been invited for an interview for the post of Administration Assistant at Fisher College. You will now need to prepare for the interview and then develop a realistic career development plan.

Task 1

You have been invited to interview and will need to **provide** appropriate responses to interview questions for the post of Administration Assistant at Fisher College.

During your interview you will need to **demonstrate** prior research and preparation when providing appropriate responses to interview questions for the post of Administration Assistant at Fisher College.

Your assessor will produce an observation statement to support your evidence.

Task 2

Produce a realistic career development plan and show evidence of the independent research and planning you have undertaken. You will need to investigate the skills, knowledge and qualifications required for your chosen career. The plan will need to be set against a realistic timescale and clearly show the steps you will need to take to achieve your career goal.

Task 3

Your final task is to **evaluate** the suitability of your career development plan.

Knowledge recap answers

Learning aim A, page 5

1. Any from: hierarchical, flat, matrix, functional, divisional.
2. Any from: sales, production, purchasing, administration, customer service, distribution, finance, human resources, ICT, marketing, research and development.
3. The marketing department carries out market research to find out if there is demand for a new product or one suggested by the R&D department. The marketing department then works with the finance department on the best way to fund a promotion for the product to ensure the business gets the right advertising without spending more than they will get back.

Learning aim A, page 8

1. The directors decide on the policies of the business, the direction it will take and changes it will need to make. The managers put those policies and actions into place.
2. The senior managers look after the target setting, planning and decisions for the **whole** business; the supervisors ensure these are carried out for **their particular** area or team.
3. Communication is important so that staff know exactly what their job is, what responsibilities they have, and how their role fits into the business. Keeping staff informed about changes will help them feel part of the business and valued. This will lead to more job satisfaction and a more efficient and profitable business.

Learning aim B, page 22

1. Any from: employee leaving, extra work (such as growth of the business), sickness, different job roles required, maternity and paternity cover.
2. It can provide the opportunity to bring new skills and knowledge into the business.
3. The job advert must not discriminate against anyone, for example by gender, ethnic origin or disability.

Learning aim B, page 23

1. The current job holder will know exactly what the job entails and will include specific requirements and skills rather than just general ones. The director is unlikely to have any recent experience of the job role.
2. Skills are about a person's ability do a job: for example, bricklaying, cooking. Qualities are about the person themselves: for example, team worker, good communicator, hard-working, organised.

Learning aim B, page 27

1. A job description contains details of the job including the job title, contract and responsibilities. A person specification contains the specific skills, experience and knowledge required to do the job.
2. The start date informs applicants when they should be available to start the job if they had to leave another one or were planning a holiday. The contract informs applicants whether it was, for example, permanent or part-time work, as this would affect their decision on whether to apply.
3. As evidence from an independent authority such as an exam board that an applicant had certain skills or knowledge that the employer required, for example, BTEC in Business.
4. Essential attributes are those skills and knowledge needed to do the job. Without these the person could not do the job and would not be considered for it. Desirable attributes are qualities an employer would like in the person so that they could do the job better and help the business progress.
5. It stands for Curriculum Vitae and is a story of your life so far including education, qualifications achieved and working towards, employment history, interests and hobbies.
6. The application form will record the same information from each applicant so this can help the employer decide whom they want to interview. In a letter and CV the applicant would only tell the employer what they wanted them to know and this might not have the information the employer wants. An application form provides a level playing field for applicants. It can also be used as a way of seeing whether people can follow instructions, such as use block capitals or blue ink.
7. Handwritten documents would show if the handwriting was clear and legible which may be an important part of the job role.
8. The job role may be physically demanding where employees are required to be able to do a lot of strenuous work. The business would test applicants to see if they were fit and would use it as a means of selecting people for the next stage of the interview process.

Learning aim C, page 49

1. You only get one chance to make a good impression on an employer and employers will be more impressed if a candidate can demonstrate they know about the business and the job role.
2. Appropriate body language includes maintaining eye contact, smiling, using a clear and positive tone of voice, active listening, showing an interest in what is happening.
3. Examples of inappropriate non-verbal behaviour include chewing gum, texting on a mobile phone, looking disinterested, being inappropriately dressed, slouching in the chair, fiddling with hair or clothes, no eye contact.

Learning aim C, page 50

1. A personal audit is to make a record of current skills, knowledge and interest to find out what sort of jobs would be suitable for you to apply for. A personal audit can identify gaps in skills and knowledge when matched against job role and person specifications. A person audit is often done using a form with a sliding scale of judgements ranging from 1 = poor to 5 = excellent.
2. A person audit could be carried out when leaving education and looking for employment or when considering a job or career change.

Learning aim C, page 54

1. Any four from: careers advice services such as Connexions, advertisements, word-of-mouth, careers fairs, friends and family, teachers, previous employers, employment agencies and government-sponsored agencies like Job Centres.
2. A career plan will help decide exactly what you want to do in your working life. The plan will identify where skills and knowledge need to be developed and how this can be done.

Picture credits

The authors and publishers would like to thank the following for the use of photographs in this volume:

Figure 1.2 © Simon Dawson/Bloomberg via Getty Images; Figure 1.3 © Kzenon – Fotolia; Figure 2.1 © M4OS Photos / Alamy; Figure 2.2 © Andrew Paterson / Alamy; Figure 3.1 © Monkey Business – Fotolia; Figure 3.2 © Odua Images – Fotolia; Figure 3.3 © auremar – Fotolia; Figure 3.4 © shotsstudio – Fotolia